THE Jethro MINISTRY

A Biblical Strategy
for Strong Teamwork

J. DALE ROACH

WESTBOW®
PRESS
A DIVISION OF THOMAS NELSON
& ZONDERVAN

New International Version (NIV) Holy Bible, New International Version®, NIV®
Copyright © 1973, 1978, 1984, 2011 by Biblica, Inc.® Used by permission.

New American Standard Bible (NASB) Copyright © 1960, 1962, 1963, 1968,
1971, 1972, 1973, 1975, 1977, 1995 by The Lockman Foundation

WestBow Press books may be ordered through booksellers or by contacting:

WestBow Press
A Division of Thomas Nelson & Zondervan
1663 Liberty Drive
Bloomington, IN 47403
www.westbowpress.com
1 (866) 928-1240

ISBN: 978-1-4908-8926-9 (sc)
ISBN: 978-1-5127-0823-3 (e)
ISBN: 978-1-4908-8927-6 (hc)

Print information available on the last page.

WestBow Press rev. date: 08/04/2015

Contents

Acknowledgments...vii

Where The Jethro Ministry Idea Began 1

Why Are We Doing What We Are Doing? 9

Biblical Foundation for Teamwork.. 15

Solo-Ministry and the Stresses of Elijah 23

The Strategy of Jesus and His Team of Disciples 31

Paul's Advice for Team Development...39

A Clear Definition of a Team 47

The Importance of a Team Leader...59

8 Attributes Needed for a High-Performance Team 79

Healthy Leadership for a New Century 85

What About the Board of Deacons?...95

Behaviors That Can Destroy The Jethro Ministry Before It Starts..... 103

The Team Ministry of Jethro Exodus 18...................................113

A Path to Team Development: 7 Basic Principles......................119

How to Build The Jethro Ministry 139

Acknowledgments

This work is dedicated to my father, the late Reverend Mr. Kenneth Roach, my grandfather, the late Reverend Mr. Clifford Roach, and my father-in-law, the late Reverend Mr. Glenn Rushing. These three wise men imparted to me a love for the Lord, His Kingdom, and the reliability of the Bible. It is my hope that all who read this work will find *The Jethro Ministry* to be true to the text of Exodus 18.

I must also express a great deal of gratitude and appreciation to the congregation of Immanuel Baptist Church, Lancaster, South Carolina. This fellowship was a pleasure to pastor. The ability of Immanuel to grow, change and seek the leadership of God was an experience of spiritual growth. This congregation was willing to say, "yes" to the idea of a new direction in ministry. They were also the first to embrace the concepts of *The Jethro Ministry*.

I would also like to express my appreciation to my brother pastors who have encouraged me to develop *The Jethro Ministry*. When speaking with them concerning this ministry, the response has been nothing but encouragement. I have a true heart for those whom God has called to serve His church. I hope that this writing will aid them as they serve the Master.

I also must thank the congregation of the First Baptist Church of Manning, South Carolina. This fellowship has taken on *The Jethro Ministry* with a deep commitment. The willingness of the deacons to embrace this strategy of taking care of God's church and working with the pastoral staff have inspired me as the Lead Pastor of this fellowship. The sincere commitment of over 200 church members in the development of *The Jethro Ministry* in its first year has proven to me once again that a church built upon the foundation of scripture will succeed.

The creation of *The Jethro Ministry* would have never taken place without the help of some very important people. There are several gifted women who have helped put this ministry strategy together. I would like to express my thanks to Judy Hammond, Camille Hiott, Lynn Berry, Joyce Pegram and Linda Pierce. Their talents, skills and love for the Lord have been a powerful resource.

Last, but certainly not least, I want to thank my wife Shelley. Her wisdom and ability to follow the Lord as my trusted partner gave me the support to "hang in there" when challenges came my way. Her constant reminding me that it is God who called me to the task of pastoring and no other has kept me faithful to the work. Saying "Thank you!" is simply not enough for such a loving and wonderful friend.

WHERE THE JETHRO MINISTRY IDEA BEGAN

Where "The Jethro Ministry" Idea Began!

■　　■　　■

*T*he *Jethro Ministry* journey began with a simple question, "How do you get church people to work together as a team?" This question was the result of several other questions.

- Why are some congregations finding it difficult to grow and prosper?
- Why are many churches not using the human resources that the Lord has created within their fellowships to become powerful for the Kingdom of God?
- Why are so many pastors and church leaders in conflict with one another?

Even though some churches would like to think that they are doing well, their character and behavior tells a different story to the world around them. Demonic forces never need to

> Demonic forces never need to visit many fellowships due to the fact that disharmony and conflict are already present.

visit many fellowships because disharmony and conflict are already present. This behavior tells the unchurched and those who have dropped out of the church that there is a problem. An atmosphere like this hinders many people from thinking about going back to church.

Several years ago I began to ask questions due to the condition of many Christian fellowships I had encountered. I saw many of my pastor friends resigning from their fellowships and several of them resigning from the ministry. I saw the behavior of congregations evolving into great issues of conflict that seemed to be fueled by disharmony and the appearance that they did not like worshipping together.

Why do many of the churches of God decline and lose hope for a healthy future? For some churches there simply is not a plan or strategy in working together. As I have witnessed this taking place over the past two decades, I came across Exodus 18 and began to read it in a different way. I began to listen to the advice of Moses' father-in-law, Jethro, in a new way. Exodus 18 opened my eyes to a strategy for ministry that I had ignored or overlooked for years. This scripture opened my heart to the plan of a very wise and godly man in creating an environment of teamwork for the people of God. Jethro's strategy and plan for Moses is simple and easy to follow.

Introducing The Jethro Ministry

"That which has been is that which will be, and that which has been done is that which will be done. So, there is nothing new under the sun." Ecclesiastes 1:9, NASB

The wisdom of Jethro is as old as the people of God. Too often older approaches are laid aside as being irrelevant for the age in which we live.

Since the time of Solomon, ideas and insights are probably the most recycled treasures that humans have. To claim that someone has a new idea carries with it a great deal of arrogance. The Jethro Ministry is not a new idea. For some, it may be a fresh approach to ministry but it is not new.

The wisdom of Jethro is as old as the people of God. Too often older approaches are laid aside as being irrelevant for the age in which we live. Some congregations along with their leadership have ignored the knowledge of ancient wisdom for the concepts of a modern-age. Jethro's wisdom has been overlooked by many congregations and replaced by ideas and procedures that have neither the power nor the design of inspired scripture. Before being able to start a journey in understanding the advice of Jethro, it will first be necessary to read the advice he gave to Moses in Exodus 18.

Exodus 18

1 Now Jethro, the priest of Midian, Moses' father-in-law, heard of all that God had done for Moses and for Israel His people, how the LORD had brought Israel out of Egypt. 2 And Jethro, Moses' father-in-law, took Moses' wife Zipporah, after he had sent her away, 3 and her two sons, of whom one was named Gershom, for he said, "I have been a sojourner in a foreign land." 4 And the other was named Eliezer, for he said, "The God of my father was my help, and delivered me from the sword of Pharaoh." 5 Then Jethro, Moses' father-in-law, came with his sons and his wife to Moses in the wilderness where he was camped, at the mount of God. 6 And he sent word to Moses, "I, your father-in-law Jethro, am coming to you with your wife and her two sons with her." 7 Then Moses went out to meet his father-in-law, and he bowed down and kissed him; and they asked each other of their welfare, and went into the tent. 8 And Moses told his father-in-law all that the LORD had done to Pharaoh and to the Egyptians for Israel's sake, all the hardship that had befallen them on the journey, and how the LORD had delivered them. 9 And Jethro rejoiced over all the goodness which the LORD had done to Israel, in delivering them from the hand of the Egyptians. 10 So Jethro said, "Blessed be the LORD who delivered you from the hand of the Egyptians and from the

hand of Pharaoh, and who delivered the people from under the hand of the Egyptians. 11 "Now I know that the LORD is greater than all the gods; indeed, it was proven when they dealt proudly against the people." 12 Then Jethro, Moses' father-in-law, took a burnt offering and sacrifices for God, and Aaron came with all the elders of Israel to eat a meal with Moses' father-in-law before God. 13 And it came about the next day that Moses sat to judge the people, and the people stood about Moses from the morning until the evening. 14 Now when Moses' father-in-law saw all that he was doing for the people, he said, "What is this thing that you are doing for the people? Why do you alone sit as judge and all the people stand about you from morning until evening?" 15 And Moses said to his father-in-law, "Because the people come to me to inquire of God. 16 "When they have a dispute, it comes to me, and I judge between a man and his neighbor, and make known the statutes of God and His laws." 17 And Moses' father-in-law said to him, "The thing that you are doing is not good. 18 "You will surely wear out, both yourself and these people who are with you, for the task is too heavy for you; you cannot do it alone. 19 "Now listen to me: I shall give you counsel, and God be with you. You be the people's representative before God, and you bring the disputes to God, 20 then teach them the statutes and the laws, and make known to them the way in which they are to walk, and the work they are to do. 21 "Furthermore, you shall select out of all the people able men who fear God, men of truth, those who hate dishonest gain; and you shall place these over them, as leaders of thousands, of hundreds, of fifties and of tens. 22 "And let them judge the people at all times; and let it be that every major dispute they will bring to you, but every minor dispute they themselves will judge. So it will be easier for you, and they will bear the burden with you. 23 "If you do this thing and God so commands you, then you will be able to endure, and all these people also will go to their place in peace." 24 So Moses listened to his father-in-law, and did all that he had said. 25 And Moses chose able men out of all Israel, and made them heads over the people, leaders of thousands, of hundreds, of fifties and of tens. 26 And they judged the people at all times; the difficult dispute they would bring to Moses, but every minor dispute they themselves would judge. 27 Then Moses bade his father-in-law farewell, and he went his way into his own land. (Exodus 18, NASB)

■   ■   ■

Jethro, the Priest of Median, asked his son-in-law two simple, yet very important questions about his behavior, "What is this you are doing?" and "Why?" These questions ignited the strategic plan of *The Jethro Ministry*.

> Knowing what we do in ministry and why we do it is crucial for survival.

These two questions combine to build a straightforward interrogation that could save lives, energy, and mental well being of many people in Christian service. Knowing what we do in ministry and why we do it is crucial for survival.

In one of the churches my father served as pastor, the ushers had an unusual practice after the offering was taken on Sunday mornings. Subsequent to the congregation giving their offerings two of the ushers would take two chairs and place them at the entrance of the sanctuary and sit in front of the doors for the rest of the worship service. This practice was unusual indeed. There were plenty of places to sit in the sanctuary; there was no further service that the men performed, but there they sat every Sunday at the back of the church in folding chairs.

The mystery proved too great for my father to refrain from inquiry. One day he broke the question. "Why do you put those chairs at the back when there are plenty of places to sit?" The response was what my father expected. "Well, Pastor I am not sure why we do it. I'll ask my father. He was taking the offering on Sundays before me." The process took some time, and the answer was slow in coming but the answer did come.

The story went back to twenty years before when a stranger had walked into the church building and disrupted the worship service. From that Sunday on, the deacons placed a guard at the entrance of the sanctuary. Although this disruption had happened only once, the pattern was set. From that day on, someone would keep guard.

Although this practice may seem somewhat silly, this is exactly how some churches perform their ministry. Many ministries build upon "old habits" that do not have a clear vision or purpose. *The Jethro Ministry* starts by asking two simple questions, "Why are we doing what we are doing?" and "Is there a better way?" Teamwork is the key to creating a successful church

> The story of Jethro is some of the best advice one can find relating to teamwork and teamwork development.

environment. The story of Jethro is some of the best advice one can find relating to teamwork and teamwork development. The following chapters use Exodus 18 as the foundation. The chapters in this book are the result of Jethro's advice to Moses. The strategy plan of Jethro can help any congregation, just as it helped Moses.

WHY ARE WE DOING WHAT WE ARE DOING?

Why Are We Doing What
We Are Doing?

■   ■   ■

In some congregations the finances, the mission work, the ministry, and the personnel resources are deployed in the same way that they have been for years. A system and format of ministry can develop and become the law of the land. No one takes the time to ask, "What are you doing?" or "Why are you doing it?" These are the questions that Jethro asked of Moses.

> The next day Moses took his seat to serve as judge for the people, and they stood around him from morning till evening. When his father-in-law saw all that Moses was doing for the people, he said, "What is this you are doing for the people? (Exodus 18:13-14a, NIV)

There will be many congregations worshiping this coming weekend in which ritual and formality override reason.

There will be many congregations worshiping this coming weekend in which ritual and formality override reason. The simple question, "What's going on here?" is never asked. As simple as this inquiry may sound, it appears to be a difficult subject for some congregations. Someone may easily tell you what programs are going on and what time to show up for events, but the question of principle and reason cannot be answered with the same kind of ease.

"Why?" was Jethro's second question for Moses. "Why do you alone sit as judge, while all these people stand around you from morning till evening?" (Exodus 18:13-14, NIV) Jethro's inquiry can be stated this way:

- What are you hoping to accomplish?
- Do you know your limitations?
- Why is everyone coming to you for advice?
- Why do you try to do this all alone?
- Why do you sit here all day and try to achieve what one man cannot possibly accomplish?

Jethro was trying to remind Moses of the fact that he was one man. The children of Israel numbered in the hundreds of thousands; one man could not handle the demands of so many by himself. In fact, one man cannot handle the needs of hundreds on his own. So, why did Moses do it by himself? His answer to Jethro was a simple one.

> Moses answered him, "Because the people come to me to seek God's will. Whenever they have a dispute, it is brought to me, and I decide between the parties and inform them of God's decrees and instructions. (Exodus 18:15-16, NIV)

The situation in which Jethro found Moses is the same in which many church leaders and members find themselves. The idea behind it is "I am *the one!*" Charles Colson in his book *The Body* speaks of the dangers of the solo leader. He says that exalting solo leadership causes those leaders to become "spiritual Lone Rangers." (Charles Colson, *The Body*, Dallas; Word Publishing, 1992, pages 296-299) This approach to ministry is not a plus for any leader within the church. It is counter-productive and in many cases self-destructive. Jethro was determined to teach this to Moses.

Before his death, I remember engaging my grandfather in a conversation during a Christmas visit in which I found his discouragement in ministry troubling. Here was a man who had given up a well paying job in his early years to become a Wesleyan pastor. His life had been dedicated to serving the Lord. In our conversation, I remember how troubled this elder saint was, concerning the lack of support he had experienced in his ministry. The theme of no support is a recurring subject within church leadership. However, I have come to believe that it is not a lack of support. It is the *organization* of support that is absent. This was the case with Moses. Able-bodied servants surrounded him, yet he ignored them while doing the tasks all-alone.

Those who have been called to serve the Lord are finding in alarming numbers that they simply cannot carry the load. The dropout rate in the ministry is a strong indicator that all is not well. There are several reasons as to why this is taking place.

> The dropout rate in the ministry is a strong indicator that all is not well.

- Many pastors do not have a true Sabbath. The idea of working seven days a week is not unusual for many ministers. Finding a day of rest is difficult for those serving in congregations.

- Some pastors have allowed the demands of their ministry to affect their personal lives with their family. There are those in church work who have placed their wife and children behind their ministry. This type of behavior is fuel for a disaster.

- Stress and conflict are problems that many were never prepared to address. How to deal with the shock and overwhelming emotions of confrontations were not taught to them in college or seminary.

- Another reason that the rates of pastor resignations and withdrawal are so high is directly connected to the care one gives to oneself. When there is no life or friendship outside of a congregation, a pastor is headed for burnout. On one occasion, Jesus turned to his disciples and said, "Come with me by yourselves to a quiet place and get some rest." (Mark 6:31)

In recent decades, the accumulating responsibilities placed upon the professional ministry have been simultaneously astounding and alarming. The load of obligations laid upon one man (or a small group of men and women) has become so overwhelming that the idea of serving the Lord in a church setting is simply unthinkable to many. Charles Colson quotes Os Guiness as saying that the pastor today is expected to be "a shrink in the pulpit, a CEO in the office, and flawless in every area of his life." (Charles Colson, *The Body*, Word Publishing; Dallas, 1992, page 297.) No one has ever said that the call to serve God is supposed to be easy. However, the enemy forces, which stand against the Kingdom of God, are doing a thorough job of making the pursuit of the call as unattractive as possible.

> Even good hearted people, who love the church, would rather their children go into any other field than see them answer the call of God as staff members of a church or to serve as missionaries.

Back in 2001 *Baptist Press* reported that about 1,400 pastors a year call a toll-free hot line of the Southern Baptist Convention, which counsels ministers through its "LeaderCare" program. According to a counselor in that program, nearly 100 SBC pastors leave their ministry every month. (Jim Brown *"Groups Seeking Causes of Alarming Clergy Dropout Rate"* March 2, 2001, Agape Press, 2001) The fashion in which some churches relate to their church staff is without a doubt affecting the desire of those of the future generation when they consider vocational ministry. The call of God can override any discouragements, but negative and destructive influence must not be ignored. Many good hearted people, who love the church, would rather their children go into any other field than see them answer the call of God as a staff member of a church or to serve as a missionary.

The scripture has an answer for the dilemma of leadership challenges. In the following chapters, the concepts of team development and team strategy for God's people will be drawn from the Old and New Testaments with emphasis upon the story of Jethro, the priest of Midian. Jesus gave evidence in His ministry that working together was the plan. The Apostle Paul also gives us New Testament support for such an approach to Kingdom work.

It can be stated that it has never been God's plan for men and women to work alone in the building of His Kingdom. Scripture gives strong evidence that God's creative design for the health and survival of mankind was for his creation to work together. The idea of working together appears to be in God's creative order and plan from the very beginning. There is a strong biblical foundation for working together in a teamwork environment.

BIBLICAL FOUNDATION FOR TEAMWORK

Biblical Foundation for Teamwork

■ ■ ■

The Bible gives references to the benefits of sharing responsibilities with others (Gal. 6:2; Rom.15:1, NASB). This sharing of responsibilities and teamwork goes as far back as the creation of Adam and Eve when God said, "It is not good for the man to be alone; I will make him a helper suitable for him." (Gen. 2:18, NASB) This scripture

> Mankind was created in the image of God who exists in an eternal triune community.

applies to much more than Adam's need for a helper or a teammate. From the beginning God intended that a man would live, play, and work with a helper. This act of God is a reflection of the Trinitarian nature of the Godhead. The Father, the Son and the Holy Spirit are a strong indication that the Creator believes in working together. Mankind is the creation of God who exists in an eternal triune community. Scripture does not support the notion of someone being isolated in God's creative order.

Development of a Team Ministry During Israel's Battle with Amalek

Moses and Israel were introduced to one of their first confrontations when they crossed paths with the Amalekites. This tribe was of the descendants of Amalek, a grandson of Esau. (John Davis, *Moses and the Gods of Egypt: Studies in Exodus*, Grand Rapids Baker Book House, 1986, page 195.) They were a fierce nomadic tribe that lived in the desert lands of the Dead Sea. Their character was that of a criminal. They were known to kill for pleasure and often raided villages to take away any booty they could carry. The worst name one called an Israelite was a "friend of Amalek." (*Life Application Study Bible*, Wheaton; Tyndale House Publishers, Inc., 1996, page 122). There can be little doubt that the Amalekites were a problem. In the recording of Israel's conflict with these people, scripture gives a vivid picture of leaders coming forward to aid Moses. These men, working together would lead Israel into victory. Their cooperation was the introduction of a team effort. Exodus chapter 17 tells the story how teamwork was engaged in the Battle of Amalek,

"The Amalekites came and attacked the Israelites at Rephidim. Moses said to Joshua, "Choose some of our men and go out to fight the Amalekites. Tomorrow I will stand on top of the hill with the staff of God in my hands."

So Joshua fought the Amalekites as Moses had ordered, and Moses, Aaron and Hur went to the top of the hill. As long as Moses held up his hands, the Israelites were winning, but whenever he lowered his hands, the Amalekites were winning. When Moses' hands grew tired, they took a stone and put it under him and he sat on it. Aaron and Hur held his hands up—one on one side, one on the other—so that his hands remained steady till sunset. So Joshua overcame the Amalekite army with the sword." (Exodus 17:8-13, NIV)

■　　■　　■

Although Moses was the leader, Joshua, Aaron, and Hur all took their places on the team in the historic and memorable battle. Moses surrendered the leadership of the fighting forces over to Joshua. Moses stood on a mountain peak and raised his staff heavenward during the battle while Aaron and Hur supported him. All four men were working for the same outcome, yet each played a different role. Moses was giving the people of God one of their first lessons in "team play." (Peter Enns, Exodus, The NIV Application Commentary, Grand Rapids: Zondervan Publishing House 2000, pages 348-349). In this story, there is a clear indication that it is God's plan to incorporate His followers into a powerful force.

The task Joshua was called to do was one of leading an army into battle. He was not to play the role of Aaron or Hur in holding up the arms of Moses. He was not called to be the mediator between Israel and God as Moses was. He was called to lead the forces of Israel into war. These actions are an example of how the various roles of teamwork figures enter the plan of God. Everyone called by God has a unique role.

The call of Joshua was to take a sword in hand. The other three men would not place their feet upon the field of battle. Diversity plays a significant

> Diversity plays a significant role in the success of God's work.

role in the success of God's work. These diversities are great, but the Holy Spirit harmonizes the work. Unity toward a cause shows great differences in character and personalities, which would lead one to agree, "oneness is not sameness." (John Moore and Ken Neff, A New Testament Blueprint for the Church, Chicago: Moody Press, 1985, page 116). A unified front can have great success with an abundance of varied gifts and skills.

One of the keys in the success of Israel over the Amalekites was the development of a *unified team*. The creation of a united front especially applied to the leader, Moses. Placing trust in those who are more skilled in particular areas is crucial for all leaders. This trust is especially important for those desiring to develop a team ministry.

One of the great calls of church leaders is to examine their strategy of leadership and ask a question similar to what Moses may have asked himself concerning Joshua: *"Do I trust this man enough to be a part of this effort?"* If team development is a goal, it is essential for the leaders of the congregation to possess a high level of trust in those they lead. The idea of shared ministry must be a model and experience for the entire congregation of God. A model for leadership cannot take place unless it begins from the top.

The support of Hur and Aaron during the battle is another clear picture of teamwork. Information about Hur is limited. He may have been the brother-in-law of Moses. Regardless of who he was, two facts stand out about Hur and Aaron during this historic battle: (1) they played a different role than Joshua, and (2) the role they played was essential to the success of Israel.

> A model for leadership cannot be accomplished unless it begins from the top.

During this battle fatigue had overwhelmed Moses. His ability to stand and hold his arms up had diminished as the battle wore on (Exodus 17:12, NASB). Moses, Hur and Aaron needed a team strategy. Jane L. Fryar says that a team effort cannot be underrated:

> "We must not underestimate the need for loyalty among members of a team. No matter the position in which an individual serves, opposition never stands far from the door. God puts His people into ministry together partly because he knows we need support from other believers as we fight the battles we will most certainly fight. No army has its soldiers trenches for one." (Jane L. Fryar, *Go and Make Disciples* (St. Louis; Concordia Publishing House, 1984, page 197.)

An image that is brought forward in the battle with Amalek is that of a praying leader. These two men undoubtedly understood how important it was for their leader to have support while he prayed. The scene gives a clear example of how the power of praying people affects the outcome of an event or struggle. A leader could benefit in receiving assistance, especially in the most crucial areas of ministry. With the assistance of Aaron and Hur, Moses was able to continue under the demands that were taxing him physically. The man of God will be glad to have assistance, and a truly spiritual leader will not resist the aide of others.

SOLO-MINISTRY AND THE STRESSES OF ELIJAH

Solo-Ministry and the
Stresses of Elijah

■ ■ ■

One of the great stories of the Old Testament deals with the prophet Elijah and his victory over the prophets of Baal on Mount Carmel (I Kings 18, NASB). Elijah experienced the ups and downs of standing as God's man in a particular place and time, but anxiety, exhaustion, fear, elation and many other emotions worked upon the prophet. Elijah experienced all these human emotions along with a victory and majesty of almighty God.

The story of Elijah will dispel the notion that negative events alone produce stress. Before Elijah challenged King Ahab and the prophets of Baal, he had experienced a wonderful, miraculous event through which God displayed his power. Elijah witnessed the actions of God in the resurrection of a dead boy (1 Kings 17:17-24, NASB).

Stress is nothing new for those who labor for God. Elijah's ministry was one of intensities. He celebrated success, disappointment, and depression within three chapters of 1 Kings. Moving from one event to another was taking a great deal of energy and strength from the great man of God. These events give witness to what can happen in ministry. There is a tendency to forget that although Elijah was a man of God, he was also very human. The challenges of Elijah's ministry were unlike the stresses most pastors and church leaders face today; however, the demands upon a leader's time are no less real or exhausting. Wayne Oates explains the types of stress that pastors face best when he says:

> The pastor moves from one crisis to another with those whom he shepherds. In a single day, he may visit the mother of a newborn baby, give guidance to a person who is becoming a Christian, talk with a high school or college graduate about his lifework, unite a couple in marriage, comfort a person who is bereaved, call upon a person who is confronting a serious operation, and listen to the last words of a patient who is dying. Two thousand years of Christian ministry have conditioned Christians to expect their pastors at these times of crisis. (Wayne E. Oates, *The Christian Pastor*, The Westminster Press, 1946, page 13)

The demands placed upon spiritual leaders are very taxing. These statements make it evident that another truth cannot be ignored: There is one thing that is certain, the Christian pastor cannot work alone. The pastor must recognize that he is not the only one who cares about the success of the church or the work of God. There is a tendency on the part of some pastors and church leaders to allow themselves to take on more than they should. When a pastor or church leader is honest with himself, he can be confident that he is not the only one who cares for the success of the kingdom of God.

> "He does not minister to his flock without soon finding that he is not the only person in the community who is concerned with the welfare of his parishioners. Nor is he alone in the depth of his devotion to people, in the clarity of his sense of mission in the world, and in the

favor of those to whom he ministers." (Wayne Oates, *The Christian Pastor*, page 139)

Wayne Oates noted in a 1973 publication that of forty-seven denominations that included both pastors and laity, "the most expected characteristic of a Christian pastor was stated as being that of an 'affirming style." (Wayne Oates, *The Christian Pastor, third edition*, Westminster Press; Philadelphia; 1973, page 17). Oates concluded that those under the leadership of the pastor expected him to be capable of handling all kinds of stressful situations by remaining calm under pressure while continuing to affirm and support them.

This expectation can cause a great deal of stress and fatigue if handled unwisely or if handled alone. The expectations placed on a leader can be extremely destructive in the life of that leader. In more recent surveys George Barna has come to these conclusions:

> The expectations placed on a leader can be extremely destructive in the life of that leader.

"Our studies show that church-goers expect their pastor to juggle an average of 16 major tasks. That's a recipe for failure - nobody can handle the wide range of responsibilities that people expect pastors to master. We find that effective pastors not only love the people to whom God allows them to minister, but also provide firm, visionary leadership and then delegate responsibilities and resources to trained believers. Ultimately, the only way a pastor can succeed in ministry is to create a team of gifted and compatible believers who work together in loving people and pursuing a commonly held vision. The pastor who strives to meet everyone's demands and tries to keep everyone happy is guaranteed to fail." (George Barna, Barna Research Group, LTD, September 25, 2001)

When Elijah encountered the prophets of Baal, there were 450 of them and an additional 400 prophetesses of Ashera (1 Kings 18:19, NASB). The odds against the prophet seemed to be overwhelming. Elijah was in direct conflict with the power of his day both in the palace and in the pagan temples. The prophet found himself facing the king and queen and their cult all alone. Although these circumstances must have seemed overwhelming, Elijah's faith was strong. It remained strong until after his great victory on Mount Carmel.

The event of Elijah taking on the pagan influences of his day is an example of how church leaders can be affected by solo ministry. Stress and despair can arise even in seasons of great success. Although the prophet had witnessed the power of God, Queen Jezebel was still an intimidating force to be reckoned with. Just

> Stress and despair can arise even in seasons of great success.

as in the case of Elijah, the taxation upon the mind, body and soul are extreme when a leader in the church faces conflicts or even successes.

Following the amazing events of a resurrected child and the defeat of the prophets of Baal, Elijah undergoes a totally different experience. He is exhausted and thoroughly drained after his overwhelming victory on Mount Carmel. He has no energy left to confront the wicked Jezebel when she threatens him (1 Kings 19:1-4, NASB). Because of his exhaustion the prophet flees to the sacred grounds of Horeb and pleads with God to take his life. He can take no more: good or bad.

The Bible indicates that the overwhelming power of God was shown on Mount Carmel and victory was strong, yet following all these events the scriptures record Elijah saying, "It is enough; now, O Lord take my life... (1 Kings 19:4a, NASB). It is in this situation that the Lord speaks to Elijah in a gentle whisper and prepares him to recruit someone to assist him. God is leading Elijah to recruit a teammate. (1 Kings 19:15-21, NASB).

In 1 Kings chapter 19 Elijah is pictured as a man who is broken and disappointed. He is found to be moping around as a solitary man lying under a small tree. Richard Nelson reflects upon Elijah's situation:

"While guessing at the psychological motivation of characters in narratives is usually a serious exegetical mistake, in this case the reader has been provided with so many explicit symptoms that the "psychologizing" process becomes inexitable! The narrative shows deep psychological insight in describing the generalized depression that sometimes results from stress in this case the stress of fear coupled with the stress brought on by victorious success." (Richard D. Nelson, *First and Second Kings*. Interpretation, page 406)

Successful ministry can indeed be stressful. It is a mistake to think that crisis and hardship are the only factors that wear on the body and spirit. Elijah had just experienced one of the greatest victories of his life when he called upon the Lord to take his life. In three short verses, the attitude of Elijah soared from extreme exhilaration relating to his victory over the prophets of Baal to a depression so deep he wished to die. In these moments the prophet is transformed from a mighty man of God to a whimpering, coward and a refugee.

This short episode in the life of Elijah is a perfect example of what can happen to those who work alone in ministry. The need to have assistance is real and must never be doubted by the believer. Elijah had to come to a point of exhaustion and depression before he discovered God's plan and design. He would soon learn that the ministry of the kingdom of God is a shared ministry.

The prophet's distress was so extreme that he flees from his victory and engages in the acts of a loser. He dismisses his servant in Beersheba (1 Kings 19:3) as if he will not need his services any longer. His journey south past Judah may also show signs that the prophet has given up and is laying aside his ministry altogether. It seems that Elijah is developing the characteristics of a man who can no longer find peace or rest. After a day's journey into the desert, an exhausted Elijah says he wants to die which ironically is the opposite desire to what he expressed by fleeing into the desert in the first place. Elijah interprets Jezebel's attacks on him as the end of it all. So far as Elijah is concerned defeat is certain. The events in chapter 19 seem to be senseless. The prophet himself becomes irrational, and his actions are confusing.

After the stresses of Mount Carmel the threat posed by Jezebel and the accompanying exhaustion, Elijah was led to a companion to help him in the remaining days of his ministry. Elijah laid his mantle upon the body of Elisha as he passed by the young man while he was working in the field. There are many interpretations as to what this action of Elijah meant. Some believe it was a symbolic transferring of the prophet's power to the young Elisha. One thing is for certain, this act of Elijah was an open and willing invitation to Elisha to become part of what God was doing.

This introduction of Elisha into the life of Elijah is another example of how the Creator wants mankind to work together. In other words, it is never the Creator's intention for his servants to work alone. The inclusion of helpers has been in God's creative order since the Garden of Eden. This also included connecting Elisha with Elijah. These two men of God were being called to combine their resources as a team.

THE STRATEGY OF JESUS AND HIS TEAM OF DISCIPLES

The Strategy of Jesus and His Team of Disciples

■ ■ ■

The life and ministerial development of Jesus and His disciples record the greatest example of a team ministry approach. He had a three-year strategy of team development that created certain behavioral patterns in His disciples and enabled them to carry on in ministry after His ascension. The development of ministry teams was not unique during the time of Christ. The scriptures teach us that before Jesus called his disciples, John the Baptist and the Pharisees also had disciples (Mark 2:18). Thus, while the calling and training of disciples was not a new concept, the way in which Jesus developed his team of disciples was exceptional.

It was clear from the beginning that Jesus had no intention of trying to do ministry alone. The ministry of Jesus started by recruiting disciples to be a part of his team. The strategy that Jesus used was one of training and deploying those he had trained to go into the world (Luke 9:1-6). The three years of Jesus'

> It was clear from the beginning that Jesus had no intention of trying to do ministry alone.

ministry was created to equip others for the task of continuing His work subsequent to his ascension.

Jesus showed that a leader must place the welfare of everyone under his or her influence as top priority. A business, volunteer group or church will never succeed if the people who make up that team feel that they are unimportant. Great leaders genuinely care for and love the people they lead more than they love the action of leading. Jesus made clear that leading others without respect and appreciation of others degenerates into self-serving and the manipulation of other people. The overall goal for any leader of any group is to assure the team members that they are of value and are trusted members with influence.

Jesus taught by his example that true leaders understand that the teams they lead are made up of very diverse individuals. This diversity can produce amazing results however; if one member of that team feels alienated or brushed aside, that team will never see its full potential. Strong leaders see diversity as complementary. Various personality traits are extremely valuable for the success of any organization. When Jesus was recruiting his team of disciples he began the process by bringing together a group of differing personalities. Although they were different, they had one purpose.

Jesus gave his disciples practical directives for the church in the Great Commission. (Matt. 28:18-20) The team that Jesus built had the purpose of spreading the gospel. Bill Hull observed that Jesus had four phases in his ministry through which he led the disciples. First was the "come and see" stage; second, was the "come and follow me" stage; third, the "come and be with me" stage: last, the "you will remain in me" stage. (Bill Hull, *Jesus Christ Disciplemaker,* Old Tappan; Fleming H. Revell Company, 1984, pages 7-12). Clearly, the intention of Christ was to develop a group of men into a ministry that would continue after his ascension.

At the beginning of His ministry, the Lord put out an invitation to His disciples to "come and see" what was taking place in His ministry. (John 1:39, 46, NASB) This leadership approach of Christ was non-threatening and gave the disciples a chance to say "no" when they found out what Jesus was about. (Matt. 19:22, NASB) According to John 1:35-51, Peter and Andrew followed Jesus at an earlier date, but then may have returned to fishing.

The expression of "following" Jesus during his ministry indicated that his disciples followed Jesus as students. Jesus showed by his example how to do the Great Commission. (Matt. 28:18-20, New American Standard Bible) He made it clear by his example what he would expect from his disciples in the future after his physical departure. In teaching his disciples about power, Jesus called them together and drew a contrast between greatness in the world and the greatness among those who belong to God (Matt 19:30, NASB). The disciples lived in a world that was dominated by the powers of Rome. Jesus intended to convey to his followers that true greatness was based on service and a willingness to sacrifice. Anyone who desired to become great must first become a servant. Jesus had an approach to leadership and teamwork that was unique from that of the world. (Mark. 9:33-37, NASB)

The phrase "follow me" is used often by the Lord (Matt. 4:19, 8:22, 9:9, 16:24, 19:21, Mk. 1:17, 2:14, 8:34, 10:21, Lk. 5:27, 9:23, 9:59, 18:22, Jn. 1:43, 10:27, 12:26, 13:36, 21:19, 21:22, NASB). This invitation was a moment when those interested in Jesus became more than spectators. They began to spend time with the Lord and His people. When Jesus encountered the rich young ruler, he used the "follow me" phrase (Matt. 19:16-22, NASB). The main objective of the Lord was not for the young man

> The disciples lived in a world that was dominated by the powers of Rome. Jesus intended to convey to his followers that true greatness was based on service and a willingness to sacrifice.

to rid himself of all his wealth. His objective was for the young man to come and "follow Me," and become part of the Lord's ministry team. The goal Christ was seeking was undivided loyalty and obedience. This phase of "following" Christ is extremely difficult for many people. The young rich man found this obedience so hard to accept that he turned and walked away. The call of Christ upon the individual for undivided loyalty is a challenge, but it is also an invitation to become part of His team.

Another truth that the story of the rich young ruler points toward is that Jesus calls for discipline in our lives that is more powerful than the security of wealth or personal success. This obedience and "following" is radical from the world's perspective. Childlike faith and loyalty to the Lord is what he seeks from those who follow Him regardless of their wealth and standing in the world. Jesus, through the working of the Holy Spirit, can reveal those areas in our lives that hinder us from following Him.

In regard to how Jesus sent out disciples, Craig A. Evans indicates that the sending out of the seventy in Luke 10 should be compared with the sending of the twelve. The sending out of the seventy was a team development strategy of Jesus to reach the world.

Some propose that the calling of the seventy was a strategy by Jesus that reflected upon an Old Testament reference. Moses appointed seventy administrators to help him in the book of Numbers. (Numbers 11:16,24, NASB) As Jesus sent the seventy out, he sent them two by two. He followed the strategy given by Moses in dealing with ministry issues: "A single witness shall not rise up against a man on account of any iniquity or any sin which he has committed; on the evidence of two or three witnesses a matter shall be confirmed." (Deut. 19:15, NASB) According to this scripture and the example of Jesus' ministry, the testimony and support of a team can prove to be reliable and trustworthy. The sending out of the seventy on their missionary journey was the first development of a team outside of the choosing of the twelve disciples. This design for ministry began at the inception of Christ's public ministry.

Jesus not only taught his disciples how to work as a team but he also gave his disciples guidance on how to handle the stresses and burdens of ministry. In Matthew chapter eleven Jesus speaks of his "yoke," an allusion to a device designed to be used upon the necks of working animals. He said,

> "Take my yoke upon you and learn from me, for I am gentle and humble in heart, and you will find rest for your souls." (Matthew 11:29, NASB)

Yokes were often used upon a single animal, but there were times when a yoke was placed upon the necks of more than one farm animal to share the task. What Christ calls for is an investment of our lives that is eternal, but not solitary. He calls his disciples to work together. As the Creator, the Lord has a clear understanding as to how people relate to one another. The design of how Jesus performed his ministry is a clear indication of team development long before the phrase "team ministry" was coined.

When Jesus began the process of calling his disciples to follow him, he began with men who had something in common. In the Gospel according to Matthew (chapter 4) the first two men that Jesus called were fishermen who also were brothers. Their names were Peter and Andrew. The next two recruits were friends of Peter and Andrew who

> The design of how Jesus performed his ministry is a clear indication of team development long before the phrase "team ministry" was coined.

were also fishermen. They were brothers whose names were James and John.

The act of Christ in recruiting the first disciples is a lesson in how important it is for any leader to begin with people who share common traits and values. These four men did not have to explain themselves to one another, neither did they have to learn each other's backgrounds. Any time a leader is attempting to build a team it is essential to have a core group of people who understand each other. This enables the establishment of stability before diversity and conflict come along. Be sure of one thing, conflict will evolve in any team effort. Before Jesus recruited the other disciples a stable core of disciples came together.

The Recruitment of the Tax Man and the Zealot

This is where the motley crew begins to expand. Can you think of anyone more different from the first four fishermen that Jesus recruited than someone who collects taxes for the Roman Empire? Matthew, the next recruit of Jesus is that man. This is a very interesting step in the recruitment process of Jesus. Not only did the fishermen probably have a dislike for Rome and the taxes they were required to pay, they most likely did not like the tax collectors. The fishermen probably had no need for Matthew. (Matthew 9:9, NASB)

If you come to realize that fishermen and a tax collector create an interesting combination, all you have to do is go to chapter 10 of Matthew's Gospel and see the full list of who Jesus called to follow him. Another interesting character is called Simon the Zealot. (Matthew 10:4) A Zealot was a member of a fanatical sect in Judea during the first century that militantly opposed the Roman domination of Palestine. If the fishermen did not like the tax collector Matthew, one can be sure that Simon (the Zealot) hated anything attached to Rome. In fact, if Simon the Zealot would have caught Matthew in a dark alley he would have most likely killed him and thought to himself, "What a great day!"

Three Basic Lessons from Jesus' Recruitment Tactics

Much can be learned from Christ in the recruitment of a productive team. *First*, begin with a core group that has something in common. (Peter, Andrew, James and John—fishermen and taxpayers to Rome) *Second*, allow diversity to be introduced to the team. It will introduce new thoughts, ideas and vision. (Matthew—tax collector for Rome) *Third*, do not fear tension and conflict. These behaviors can produce great results if handled well. (Simon the Zealot—hater of Rome)

These are just a few of the lessons that Jesus taught "by what he did rather than what he said." Strong teams are built upon diversity. In fact, a group of people like this can do great things together. It is all about working together even in our diversities. A strong leader also places commitment to one another as a must. Granted, members of the team may never become best friends but their loyalty and commitment to the overall cause is essential. This will only take place when the team leader sets an example of allegiance and trust with every member of the team. Jesus was not only the greatest Teacher known to mankind, he also showed His wisdom and power by the way he recruited his team of disciples.

PAUL'S ADVICE FOR TEAM DEVELOPMENT

Paul's Advice for Team Development

■ ■ ■

In the development of healthy, strong teamwork, leaders must convey a clear understanding that teams are a powerful human resource of varied talents. Groups of diverse individuals brought together whether as employees, volunteers, or church organizations create powerful resources. Although this creation is true there is a challenge that faces every team in its early stages. A leader's challenge must focus on the discovery of the personal talents of those on the team. This discovery of talents was the goal of the New Testament Church leader, the Apostle Paul.

One of the greatest challenges for developing a strong team is finding out what makes every person on the team "tick." Some people are born knowing what they want to do in life. Their purpose in life does not have to be explained or defined for them. Others have great skills and talents but simply do not know what to do with their abilities. If a group is going to be healthy and strong there must be a process of talent discovery.

> A leader's challenge must focus on the discovery of the personal talents of those on the team.

Talent discovery is not an easy process, but talents can be revealed by asking a few questions. Here are just a few questions to consider when helping someone find his or her place on the team.

Is this person a *people person*?
Is this person a *project person*?
Is this person a *product person*?
Is this person a *problem solving person*?

These questions may sound simple and basic, but these four questions can help any leader in clarifying what the members of the team enjoy doing the most? One of the worst experiences of any organization is to place someone in a place where they simply do not belong. Another problem is to expect one person to be all four of the "talents" listed above. Strong teams are made up of various people with different skills working for a common purpose. The discovery of talents for any team takes time, effort, and a great deal of patience. A good leader knows this.

Diversity is a Strong Resource

One of the reasons some organizations, businesses and churches are declining is due to ignoring the energy of different ideas, concepts and convictions. For any group to see its full potential, it must first respect the differences of those who make up the team. This respect does not mean that convictions or ideologies are watered down. It simply means that the uniqueness of others on the team is acknowledged and respected. The Apostle Paul sought out the unique characteristics and differences of early church members. Diversity is a great resource!

The Apostle Paul's Understanding of Teamwork

In the writings of Paul, one of his strongest descriptions of the church is that of the church as the body of Christ (1 Cor. 12:27, NASB). A human body functioning in a healthy way means that all of its constituent organs are working properly and together. Likewise, the body of Christ cannot be healthy without the proper orchestration of its various parts. This concept of unity and oneness began with the teaching of Jesus.

The creation of oneness is accomplished by encouraging the use of the individual gifts of the believers. Every Christian possesses a spiritual gift to use in a team effort. The giving of the various gifts had

> The major goal of diverse gifts is to build a healthy body, a unified team.

a significant purpose, which was to unify the body of Christ. Paul desired to recognize the diversity of church members yet acknowledge Christ as Lord regardless of the gift (Eph. 4:12, NASB). The major goal of diverse gifts is to build a healthy body and unified team.

In 1 Corinthians 12:12-31 Paul dealt with a diversity in the body of Christ as well as its unity. Paul's overriding theme in this letter is *unity in diversity*. The development of a team approach to ministry must be carefully guided because the unity of the church must override its diversity. Teamwork is essential for the survival of a healthy fellowship. The Apostle Paul put this way in 1st Corinthians chapter 12,

> "Now about the gifts of the Spirit, brothers and sisters, I do not want you to be uninformed. You know that when you were pagans, somehow or other you were influenced and led astray to mute idols. Therefore, I want you to know that no one who is speaking by the Spirit of God says, "Jesus be cursed," and no one can say, "Jesus is Lord," except by the Holy Spirit.
>
> There are different kinds of gifts, but the same Spirit distributes them. There are different kinds of service, but the same Lord. There are different kinds of working, but in all of them and in everyone it is the same God at work.
>
> Now to each one the manifestation of the Spirit is given for the common good. To one there is given through

the Spirit a message of wisdom, to another a message of knowledge by means of the same Spirit, to another faith by the same Spirit, to another gifts of healing by that one Spirit, to another miraculous powers, to another prophecy, to another distinguishing between spirits, to another speaking in different kinds of tongues, and to still another the interpretation of tongues. All these are the work of one and the same Spirit, and he distributes them to each one, just as he determines.

Just as a body, though one has many parts, but all its many parts form one body, so it is with Christ. For we were all baptized by one Spirit so as to form one body—whether Jews or Gentiles, slave or free—and we were all given the one Spirit to drink. Even so the body is not made up of one part but of many.

Now if the foot should say, "Because I am not a hand, I do not belong to the body," it would not for that reason stop being part of the body. And if the ear should say, "Because I am not an eye, I do not belong to the body," it would not for that reason stop being part of the body. If the whole body were an eye, where would the sense of hearing be? If the whole body were an ear, where would the sense of smell be? But in fact God has placed the parts in the body, every one of them, just as he wanted them to be. If they were all one part, where would the body be? As it is, there are many parts, but one body

The eye cannot say to the hand, "I don't need you!" And the head cannot say to the feet, "I don't need you!" On the contrary, those parts of the body that seem to be weaker are indispensable, and the parts that we think are less honorable we treat with special honor. And the parts that are unpresentable are treated with special modesty, while our presentable parts need no special treatment. But God has put the body together, giving greater honor to the parts that lacked it, so that there should be no division in the body, but that its parts should have equal concern for each other. If one part suffers, every part suffers with it; if one part is honored, every part rejoices with it.

Now you are the body of Christ, and each one of you is a part of it." (1st Corinthians 12:1-27, NIV)

The notion that the body could function without unified body parts would be unacceptable to Paul. A body of believers functioning outside of a team structure would be foreign to Paul's understanding of the church.

> A body of believers functioning outside of a team structure would be foreign to Paul's understanding of the church.

Here are four more suggestions for those who wish to engage in healthy team ministry. Before you can apply these suggestions, you must understand that God's intention is for personal ministries to take place in interpersonal settings. Institutionalism dominates the ministry framework of many congregations. Battling behavior of this nature is why Paul referred to the first century church as the body of Christ. Suggestions for a close team ministry are:

1. Build the congregation as a community of personal relationships;
2. Visualize for the congregation the kinds of ministry that can take place as interpersonal rather than institutional functions;
3. Encourage the building of relationships with non-Christians as a context for ministry; and
4. Encourage the body to form supportive teams for their personal ministries. (Lawrence O. Richard and Gilbert R. Martin, *Lay Ministry*, page 204).

The development of personal and supportive teams makes it possible for any congregation to expand its ministry throughout its fellowship into the world. Establishing a healthy teamwork environment based upon the Bible will grow a strong fellowship. The story of Moses and the advice of his father-in-law, Jethro, can prove to be a useful team-building tool. The Apostle Paul also understood how important it is for the church to function, in harmony as a living organism. Teamwork is a strategy created thousands of years ago that can be a powerful tool for the modern church.

A CLEAR DEFINITION
OF A TEAM

A Clear Definition of a Team

■   ■   ■

A team is "a group of people trained or organized to work together." Defining the team concept will vary from author to author. However, there are three basic foundational principles that can be used to define a team.

First, the team is a collaborative approach designed to accomplish the task(s) at hand. The primary focus of any team is to work in partnership for a common goal or cause. A collaborative approach assumes that there is a desire to work together towards a common cause. Numerous organizations have failed because they did not consider the character or the desires of their work force to work in partnership:

> A collaborative approach assumes that there is a desire to work together towards a common cause.

"Our society has moved from the formalistic to the collaborative. Today, those who work in organizations demand a chance to be involved, and they expect to have their talents and skills utilized effectively; they are also willing to participate in activities that will make the organization perform more effectively. Because it has become generally accepted that creativity and innovation are traits widely distributed through the population, managers must be able to discover and put to use the resources within their teams. Once creative forces are unleashed within an organization, the potential for positive results is greatly enhanced." (Glenn H. Varney, *Building Productive Teams*, San Francisco; Jossey-Bass Publishers 1989, 2)

Second, an important issue in dealing with team development is a commitment. Commitment must begin with the team leader. Without the commitment from the leadership, a healthy team will be difficult if not impossible to build and maintain. According to William G. Dyer, commitment is the most critical factor in team development. He says:

"I feel commitment increases if people know what is going to happen and if the process makes sense. But after reviewing the approach and providing all the insight I can, then I want to know about people's commitment. For me, testing commitment is an art, not a science. I cannot measure whether a person is a 6 or an 8 on a commitment scale, because I do not have a scale. I have to talk and listen to others talk and trust my experience and judgment. I judge commitment, to some degree, by the willingness of the leader and unit members to take responsibility for team-building work, to spend time, to accept assignments, and to get involved in the agreed-on actions. Team building is a human process. It involves human feelings, attitudes, and actions. It is something that people have to accomplish among themselves. You cannot substitute high-paid consultants, complex designs, or fancy resorts for human beings making a mutual commitment to try to work together more effectively." (William G.

Dyer, *Team Building*, Massachusetts; Addison-Wesley
Publishing Company, 1987, x)

The value of personal commitment is important. The strength of any organization will depend upon the level of commitment of each member. The commitment of the team leader is foundational in the development of the team member's attitude.

Third, the team is a coordination of individual talents into a corporate whole. Thus, the major goal of anyone developing a team must be to consider the needs of those working within the group if the team is to be successful.

> The dynamics of cooperation and competition have been shown to affect attitudes and productivity. A meta-analysis confirms that cooperative experiences as compared to competitive experiences, reduce prejudice, increase acceptance of others, and heighten morale. Traditionally, competition has been assumed to motivate productivity. However, meta-analyses clearly indicate that cooperation induces higher achievement and productivity, especially on more complex tasks and problems that benefit from the sharing of information and ideas. (Richard Guzzo, Eduardo Salas and Associates, *Team Effectiveness And Decision Making In Organizations*, San Francisco; Jossey-Bass Publishers, 1995, 89)

These three words: ***collaboration, commitment,*** and ***coordination*** are foundational for the definition of team ministry. In designing a team these three building blocks can enable the team leader to define and create directives that are clear and aimed toward a productive future. When Jethro came to Moses to give him advice, collaboration, commitment and

> When Jethro came to Moses to give him advice, collaboration, commitment and coordination of God's people was his suggestion.

50

coordination of God's people was his suggestion. These three actions of a leader can create a teamwork environment that includes the God-given gifts of everyone.

Sharing a Vision

One of the greatest challenges any leader has in regard to team development is the clarifying of a vision. Without a clear vision, the leader is crippled in developing a team concept. Vision and team development are evolutionary processes. According to Wellin, Byham, and Wilson:

> "In an empowered organization, the best guidance comes from the team's understanding of the organization's vision and values. It cannot come from the rules or books of procedure; that is not empowerment. No book of procedures can answer all the questions that arise, and manuals are quickly outdated. The vision of the organization tells the team in which direction the organization is going and what it plans to accomplish. The organization's values tell the team how to accomplish the vision. Values are the subtle control mechanisms that informally sanction or prohibit behavior." (Richard S. Wellins, William C. Byham, and Heanne M. Wilson, Empowered Change (San Francisco; Jossey-Bass Publishers, 1991, 78)

A vision is a believable, credible and attractive future for a team, organization, or congregation. A vision attempts to define a distinct future. Sharing a unified vision creates a clear definition for an organization. Burt Nanus gives a clear and concise definition: "A vision is only an idea or an image of a more desirable future for the organization, but the right vision is an idea so energizing that it, in effect, jump-starts the future by calling forth skills, talents, and resources to make it happen." (Burt Nanus, *Visionary Leadership*, San Francisco, Jossey Bass, Publishers,

1992, 8) The advice of Jethro to Moses was that of a visionary. Jethro saw something that Moses did not see. Jethro's goal was to help Moses see the unseen. Jethro led Moses to see a vision and to define that vision. In support of his definition of vision Nanus gives four accommodating foundational statements:

- The right vision attracts commitment and energizes people.
- The right vision creates meaning in workers' lives.
- The right vision establishes a standard of excellence.
- The right vision bridges the present and future. (Visionary Leadership, pp.15-19)

To build upon the vision, those who are in leadership must entrust the development of that vision to others. The "how-to's" of a vision must be released to others for successful accomplishment of the vision. (Richard S. Wellins, William C. Byham, and Heanne M. Wilson, *Empowered Change,* San Francisco: Jossey-Bass Publishers, 1991, 93)

According to Reggie McNeal, a true leader leads from the future. Vision, in other words, is the domain of true leaders. The visionary does not live in the past but rather seeks to create a new future. Thus, McNeal observes that a true visionary is one who does not accept the present as the conclusion, but is rather "drawing up plans and supervising bridge-building projects to link the present with a better future they have seen." (Reggie McNeal, *Revolution In Leadership,* Nashville; Abingdon Press, 1998, 82)

Likewise Bob Dale adds to the definition and purpose of a leader and his/her vision when he writes:

The first task of the leader. . . is to focus the group's vision. Leaders help followers become more conscious of their own needs, values, self-definition, and purposes. Leaders serve their followers instead of the other way around. The act of consciousness raising calls for an unusual level of self-differentiation on the part of the leaders. (Bob Dale,

Good News From Great Leaders, New Your; The Alban Institute, 1992, 7)

The vision of the leader along with his values provides what Dale says is the rudder that "keeps their emotional and spiritual ships steady and on course." (*Good News From Great Leaders*, 7)

A common and shared vision also unites any team. Attempting to develop a team without a unifying vision is difficult if not impossible. Team leadership calls upon the leader to set the standard for the team. In short, a leader's success in establishing a team-based organization will demand a high level of commitment to the task and the people who make up the team.

The Evolution of a Group into a Team

When people are invited to work together, they initially are no more than a group that lacks a common purpose and do not share any responsibility for one another or the cause. On a performance level, this coming together is no more than a collection of people with different opinions and goals. If a collection of individuals stays together, they may evolve into a group. The difference between a group and a collection of people can be defined in their behavior and their interaction with one another. The group has come to a point in which they identify a common purpose:

> "Members develop a group identity, define their roles, clarify their purpose, and establish norms for working together. However, groups tend to be leader-centered; the leader provides direction, assigns tasks, reviews performance, and is the primary focus of communication." (Steve Buchholz, Thomas Roth and Karen Hess, Creating the High Performance Team, New York: John Wiley and Sons, 1987, 15-16)

If a group remains in this phase, the chances for the creativity and input of the entire team will never be realized. Teams cannot evolve until there is a collection of individuals that develop group ideologies and goals. A team is not easy to develop, but the evolution of teams enables a group to focus energy, respond rapidly to opportunities, and share both responsibilities and rewards. When a team is purpose-centered the members not only understand the purpose but also commit and use that purpose to guide the actions and decisions of their organization.

Dynamics of Successful Teamwork

In the development of successful teams, certain freedoms must be given to those individuals who make up the team. The development of a team leads members to use their insights and creativity. The freedom given to team members to use their creativity demands that the team leader grant trust and confidence to those with whom he is working. This trust will also call upon the team leader to have a level of courage that can withstand the possibility of failure. (Frances Hesselbein; Marshall Goldsmith; Richard Beckhard, *The Organization of the Future,* San Francisco; Jossey-Bass Publisher, 1997, 298)

There are a number of strong indicators that suggest that a team mentality is developing within an organization. One such sign can be observed in the powers allotted to the organization by its leaders. Trust of those being led is key. Jethro made it clear to Moses that he would have to trust other men to help him take care of the people of God.

When the leadership of an organization or congregation becomes more aware of the creativity and the spontaneity of the group over their own skills, team development is headed into a strong growth pattern. (Glen H. Varney, *Building Productive Teams,* (San Francisco; Jossey-Bass Publishers, 1989, 2) Such trust and freedom will encourage the group to grow in the

> Jethro encouraged Moses to find men of faith, trust them and allow them to lead.

practice of exercising individual insights and knowledge. In the story of Jethro's advice, it is obvious that Moses had a deep appreciation for his father-in-law's influence. Jethro encouraged Moses to find men of faith, trust them and allow them to lead. This level of trust passed to the team by the team leader will develop an extremely productive behavior of "brainstorming."

Brainstorming

Brainstorming is a method that generates imaginative and creative solutions to the problem. With this method, members are encouraged to come up with extreme and in some cases, outlandish methods of solving problems and creating strategies. They are encouraged to build on one another's ideas. Destructive criticism of any ideas generated is forbidden. Through this process, members see their individual contribution entering into the decision-making process and thus tend to be more accepting of the final decisions. (Varney, *Building Productive Teams*, 82)

When a team leader encourages the sharing of ideas and creativity among those he is leading, the group expands beyond itself. Brainstorming is a process that can bring out the creative, hidden talents of the team, and the collective resources of the group are always much greater than that of any one person. Jethro knew this to be true when he encouraged Moses to select several men to help him care for the children of Israel.

Each team member has a vast store of ideas available at any given moment. Regrettably, this resource often goes untapped. Using the dynamics of the group, one can create a flurry of activity. The result is frequently the unleashing of the team's collective creativity, skills and abilities. Jethro began giving Moses council by asking him a question rather than telling him the solution. (Exodus 18:18, NASB)

Buchholz, Roth and Hess offer six basic guidelines to aid an organization in the brainstorming process. First, go for quantity rather than quality. The goal in any brainstorming situation is to bring forth as many ideas and visions as possible, not to stifle the team. Second, effective brainstorming must have time limits. The limit of time will act as a motivation for people to think more rapidly and be more extensive in their thought process. Third, an effort should be made to include all ideas. The sharing of all ideas, no matter how outlandish they may be, is important at this point in team development. Fourth, it is essential to keep a record of all the brainstorming that is taking place by writing it down. A record of all ideas will provide a reference to call upon at a later date. The fifth guideline given by the three authors is unique: the leader of a team is called upon to be childlike. To be childlike in a seeking and experimental way is a constructive character trait to possess; conversely, to be childish, selfish and self-centered is a destructive trait. "One good way to judge the success of a brainstorming session is by how much laughter rings out." (Steve Buchholz; Thomas Roth; Karen Hess, eds, *Creating the High Performance Team*, 143) Having a sense of humor is absolutely necessary for any teamwork. Laughter will enhance the sessions and create a relaxing atmosphere for creativity. Jehtro recognized that Moses was under great stress. The ability of Moses to laugh and enjoy life was most likely absent. The advice of his father-in-law was not only one of organization but also one of protection for Moses.

If a church desires to engage in *The Jethro Ministry* it must first work toward becoming the best team possible. To achieve this it will require that a collaborative, committed and coordinated ministry be established. This will require the four basic principles discussed in this chapter: 1) Sharing a Vision, 2) Evolving from a Group into a Team, 3) Understanding the Dynamics of Successful Teamwork and 4) Being willing to Brainstorm.

Finally, those involved in *The Jethro Ministry* must have a vision for this ministry to succeed. It will have to be a priority. There also must be a desire to see this ministry evolve. It will call for changes and adjustments as it grows. It cannot be seen as another church program that will be put on the shelf in two or three years. There must be a desire within the church leadership to grow and see success in *The Jethro Ministry*. This can take place only when the fellowship seeks to understand what successful teamwork looks like. All these things occur when seeking the guidance of the Lord is an active part of the ministry. Allowing the Holy Spirit to speak to our minds and our hearts is essential. Constantly seeking the guidance and revelation of the living God is a must. A clear definition of teamwork will never grow without seeking the Lord's guidance through prayer and commitment as a team leader.

THE IMPORTANCE
OF A TEAM LEADER

The Importance of a Team Leader

■ ■ ■

The commitment of the leader of a team must precede the commitment of those who follow. In fact, leadership development must become a personal priority of the leader before others will follow:

> "In effect, you have decided to lead yourself. This commitment allows you to see the opportunity that could be present in leading others. It also allows others to see you as a potential leader. The huge commitment that can be involved in leading is what causes many of us to draw back from it." (Geoffrey M. Bellman, *Getting Things Done When You Are Not In Charge*, San Francisco: Berrett-Koehler Publishers, 1992, page 18)

> Most leaders do not hold back because they do not know how to lead, but because they wonder if the vision will continue to be important to them.
> **Geoffrey M. Bellman**

Many leaders' failure to provide strong leadership is not necessarily because they do not know how to lead. The major issue for long-term leadership is not talent but rather an issue of importance. The struggle that many leaders deal with evolves from their own personal commitment. This statement brings up the issue of dedication. Is the investment worth the leader's time and participation?

Dreams and visions for any organization are frequently never realized because of short-term investing and a narrow view of what is in the future. The fact that a leader does not have a dream becomes obvious to those whom he is trying to lead. Dreaming and sharing dreams take time to develop.

One of the primary functions of a leader is to help create and encourage energy within the organization he leads. Another area that is influenced by a committed leader is that of energizing those with whom he works. If one's leadership does not result in giving people more energy, then one is not a real leader.

Stability in leadership is extremely important, so the changing of leadership on the team could cause problems for any organization. The tenure of leaders or the lack of tenure can be connected to the successes or problems of the organization, charity group, volunteer team and a congregation.

As teams develop, it is essential that the team managers give each member enough authority to work and manage their own processes. This allowance should increase as the team matures and gains confidence in their mission and tasks. If a leader does not allow his authority and leadership to convey confidence to those he is leading, then the results will be negative.

When overpowering authority or leadership intervenes in a team, it can affect the team by (1) throwing the team off track, (2) decreasing the motivation of the team, (3) reducing the commitment of the team members, and (4) causing more problems than solutions. (J. Richard Hackman, Groups That Work, San Francisco: Jossey-Bass Publishers, 1990, page 485) The healthiest way for a leader to work with those he is trying to lead is through influence. The development of influence takes time and requires being trusted by the team.

Motivation of a Team

Authority is allowed under the umbrella of influence. The influence of a healthy leader can be profound and extensive. Influence carries broader implications than authority. (Gene W. Dalton, Louis B. Barnes, Abraham Zaleznik, *The Distribution of Authority In Formal Organizations*, page 37) A high-quality leader is anyone who chooses to set a positive example for others to follow.

> A high-quality leader is anyone who chooses to set a positive example for others to follow.

Teams choose to respond positively or negatively to the issues they face. They can never motivate anyone; people must motivate themselves. Therefore, "the role of the team leader is to create the kind of environment that will allow people to motivate themselves." ("*Involvement Skills for Team Leaders: A Special Presentation for Springs Industries*", page 17) This type of environment, one of trust, was what Jethro encouraged Moses to create.

The ultimate responsibility of the team leader is to help in the development of an environment in which a person can become motivated. This motivation will encourage those who are being led to be challenged in interesting work, to set goals and monitor their achievements, and to share opinions, observations, ideas and vision. This behavior will call upon the team leader to give up responsibilities so he can provide support to the team when possible. The team leader must become a coach for the organization. This was exactly what Jethro was leading Moses to become – a coach. Without the sharing of responsibilities Jethro was certain that Moses was headed toward failure and burnout.

Burnout and Its Effects Upon Team Leaders

> It is a mistake to believe that "burnout" is anything new. The results of physical, spiritual, and mental stress upon God's people and leaders have been around for centuries.

"Burnout" is a word that has become part of the common vocabulary of the work force

62

of American culture. According to Barry Farber, "the concept of burnout was born in the early 1970's, its heritage embedded in the ideas and efforts of Herbert Freudenberger in New York and Christina Maslach and Ayala Pines in California." (Barry A. Farber, ed., *Stress and Burnout in the Human Service Professions*, Pergamon Press, 1983, IX preface) A general definition of burnout is "a latent process of psychological erosion resulting from prolonged exposure to job stress." (Wilmar B. Schaufeli, Christina Maslach and Tadeusz Marek, editors, *Professional Burnout: Recent Developments in Theory and Research*, Taylor and Francis; Washington, D.C.; 1993, page 10) If this definition is accurate, then God's people suffered from stress under the hands of Pharaoh and the institution of slavery. It is a mistake to believe that "burnout" is anything new. The results of physical, spiritual, and mental stress upon God's people and leaders have been around for centuries.

The stressful experiences of life obviously have an effect upon our lives. Pines, Aronson, and Kafry, in their joint efforts to define "burnout" give insightful information relating to the subject:

> Lack of control over one's environment is a highly stressful experience. Martin Seligman suggested that when animals and people repeatedly undergo negative experiences over which they have no control, the result is "learned helplessness" and depression. The exposure to uncontrollable events leads to motivational and effective debilitation . . ., for example [those] subjects who were given unsolvable anagrams later could not solve solvable anagrams, and subjects who were exposed to inescapable noise did not attempt to escape later when escape was possible. People who develop "learned helplessness" do not believe that success is the result of their performance but attribute failure to themselves. They develop low self-esteem and become passive and sad. (Anayal M. Pines,

Elliott Aronson and Ditsa Kafry, *Burnout,* The Free Press; New York, 1981), pages 69-70)

As stated earlier, burnout is not a new phenomenon. For instance, at various times burnout has been equated with tedium, stress, dissatisfaction, professional depression, alienation, low morale, anxiety, strain, tension, feeling worn out, experiencing flame out, tensions, conflict, pressure, nerves, boredom, chronic or emotional fatigue, poor mental health, crisis, helplessness, vital exhaustion, and hopelessness. (Anayal M. Pines, Elliot Aronson, Ditsa Kafy, *Burnout,* New York: The Free Press, 1981, pages 69-70) Regardless of what title one places upon burnout, there are a few facts that are true. Burnout is a negative state that affects a person physically, emotionally, mentally and spiritually. These effects lead to exhaustion as the end result, and exhaustion most often leads the person affected into a state of disillusionment. This behavior is found most often among highly motivated people who work in emotionally and physically demanding situations. (Schaufeli, Maslach, and Marek, *Professional Burnout,* page 9)

Hans Selye identifies three stages in the development of burnout. First is the "alarm" stage, or what is called the "fight or flight" stage. This stage of alarm begins when anyone faces a challenge or a conflicting situation. The next stage is what Selye calls the "resistance" stage, which has a longer life span than the "fight or flight" stage. It is also the stage in which a person deals with issues more on a psychological basis. The third and final stage is what Selye refers to as the "exhaustion" stage. During this stage the alarm stage reappears and causes extreme fatigue, disease, disability and even death. (Wendell L. French, Fremont E. Kast and James E. Rosenzweiz, *Understanding Human Behavior in Organizations,* Harper & Row Publishers; New York, 1985, pages 650-651)

Not only are there the personal emotions of stress and burnout but also there are the cultural ones as well. Burnout and stress can even be brought on by the events that take place outside people's circle of influence and direct involvement. Clive T. Goodworth lists six causes of stress. Those stressors are:

1. The pressure of a technological age: Traditionally our forebears spent most of their lives working at means rather than ends. Modern technology permits us to obtain these ends with minimal effort.
2. Living in an era of increasing lawlessness and violence
3. Being a cog in the gigantic machine of life
4. The waning of religion and tradition
5. The stress of political disunity
6. Terrorism

    (Clive T. Goodworth, *Taking the Strain*, Hatchinson Business; London, 1986, pages 6-10)

Jethro came to Moses and warned him that if he continued to take care of God's people all by himself that he was headed toward total exhaustion. He said, ""What you are doing is not good. You and these people who come to you will only wear yourselves out. The work is too heavy for you; you cannot handle it alone." (Exodus 18:17-18, NIV) This was an early warning in God's word about burnout.

Jethro had obviously seen "burnout" a long time before anyone in the 1900's coined the phrase. Jethro's conversation with Moses came from a life of experience. He had an understanding that spiritual leaders needed to be taught how to take care of themselves and the people of God. This skill is not something that a leader automatically knows, but it is

> Burnout is a real problem for many leaders and participants of church work.

something that must be sought out and organized within the church not only with pastor but also with all members of the church. Burnout is a real problem for many leaders and participants of church work.

Burnout, physical and mental exhaustion have been around for some time. If not addressed burnout can lead to depression and extreme fatigue. Esther Schubert wrote about this problem when addressing the problems that missionaries deal with. (*What Missionaries Need to Know About Burnout and Depression*, Olive Branch Publication, New

Castle, Indiana, 1993). Burnout and some cases of depression can be prevented. Here are ten ways that Schubert suggests for burnout prevention:

1. Learning to "off load" emotionally. This requires being in touch with ones own feelings, keeping short accounts, not allowing grudges and frustrations to build up in personal relationships, and dealing with issues as they occur.

2. Learning to say "no" when one is asked to do more than is reasonable.

3. Being alert to desperate feelings and understanding the emotional implications of those feelings. It may help to consider a "worst-case" scenario to defuse the subliminal unconscious fears. This will help any person confront the "what if" and to acknowledge the adequacy of God's grace.

4. Eating a regular and balanced diet is certainly a great resource for good health and burnout prevention.

5. Making time for meaningful relationships and fellowship is necessary.

6. Keeping the capacity for laughter alive. Remember "A merry heart doeth good like a medicine!"

7. Exercise. Good exercise releases body chemicals called endorphins that lift the mood and help in preventing depression.

8. Devotional Life. A strong prayer life provides us with encouragement. It creates a sense of God's presence in our good times as well as our bad and challenging times.

9. Sleep Patterns. We must never forget that God is far more interested in us than He is in our work habits. We are not God's pets; we are his "beloved." If we wear ourselves out we will miss a wonderful opportunity of fellowship with the Lord. Self-destruction was not in His creative design.

10. Honoring the Sabbath and remembering all of creation is geared to one day of rest per week. Never forget that the Creator of the Universe took a day off himself.

These ten points can help prevent burnout from taking place. However, the first step is to acknowledge what is important to you. If you can understand that burnout and exhaustion were not part of God's plan for your life, this will be the first step to avoiding it. The sharing of responsibilities is key for reducing burnout. As G. R. Collins notes, "the belief that no one else can help is a sure road to burnout." (G. R. Collins, *"How to handle burnout"* Christian Herald, December 1979, pages 17-20) Support and close contact with others are needed to prevent burnout.

Burnout is a tool that Satan uses to destroy the people of God. It works against the design and plan of God for His people. Consider these statements when dealing with the temptation to exhaust your mental, spiritual, and physical resources:

- Stress means stretching yourself beyond your limits, overextending yourselves without an adequate time for recovery.
- When you worry about or obsess over unavoidable future events and are preoccupied with them even after they have passed, that's stress. If you have something in your life that's dominating your thinking that you cannot release, that's an indication that it is stressful.
- In life, valleys of recovery should follow mountains of high stress levels.
- When you go from one mountain to another with no time to relax and you don't deal with your stress, burnout occurs.
- Burnout means to deplete oneself...to wear oneself out by striving to reach unrealistic expectations imposed by self, values of the society or your church. (National Preschool and Children's Convention, Oct. 16-19 at LifeWay Christian Resources of the Southern Baptist Convention, Norm Wright)

Churches can also implement remedies to prevent tedium and burnout among their members. A reduction in the number of people for whom one person has responsibilities is advisable and healthy, as well as making time available for oneself and others to have downtime. This is the strategy of The Jethro Ministry. The amount of stress-related work should also be monitored and organized. Stress and burnout can be prevented with adequate training for the tasks at hand. An organization does employees and team members a favor by making the working conditions positive and by making the work significant. Jethro clearly observed what was taking place with Moses. His advice to Moses was to create an environment of teamwork that would stop exhaustion and fatigue before it took place and, thus, help him grow as a leader.

There are many who refer to themselves as leaders yet they do not possess the skills that are required to lead. The foundation of any true leader is to help others reach their full talents and potential. Leadership is not about self, but rather it is all about those who are being led. Leadership is much more than being someone in charge or control. Leading others is not achieved by holding a certain name or title. Nor is it gained by presenting one's self as an energetic personality to be followed. Leadership is not determined by how much charisma one possesses. Effective leadership aims to create an environment of trust. If the goal is gaining the trust of others to follow you, how is this accomplished?

Leadership is All about Character

A team will never become more than the leader. This calls for leaders to examine themselves and be sure that their goals, purposes and intentions are pure and straightforward. When leaders show honesty and truthfulness to those they lead, leaders build a support system that cannot be bought. For this to take place, a leader must know who they are. The questionnaire below can help a leader avoid burnout and stress by discovering themselves.

What Kind of Leader are You?

Do you know what kind of leader you are? Do you know your leadership skills? Are you able to convey your leadership styles? Answer each question then follow the instructions at the bottom of this questionnaire. Be honest, for the best results!

1. I do not expect those I lead to be creative.
    Agree 1 2 3 4 5 6 7 8 9 10 Disagree

2. Every team needs an administration, policy-making group.
    Agree 1 2 3 4 5 6 7 8 9 10 Disagree

3. A majority must lead the team.
    Agree 1 2 3 4 5 6 7 8 9 10 Disagree

4. The team leader must generate the vision of the team.
    Agree 1 2 3 4 5 6 7 8 9 10 Disagree

5. The leader's responsibility is to approve all important decisions.
    Agree 1 2 3 4 5 6 7 8 9 10 Disagree

6. The team should have a hierarchy of authority.
    Agree 1 2 3 4 5 6 7 8 9 10 Disagree

7. The leadership of the team should be equally shared.
    Agree 1 2 3 4 5 6 7 8 9 10 Disagree

8. Team success should be assessed by quality rather than by quantity.
    Agree 1 2 3 4 5 6 7 8 9 10 Disagree

9. I do not feel a need to be accountable to anyone for my leadership decisions.
    Agree 1 2 3 4 5 6 7 8 9 10 Disagree

10. The successful team must be driven by a well-defined administration.
    Agree 1 2 3 4 5 6 7 8 9 10 Disagree

11. There should be no leadership distinctions among the members of a team.
    Agree 1 2 3 4 5 6 7 8 9 10 Disagree

12. I have a strong desire to help others become leaders.
    Agree 1 2 3 4 5 6 7 8 9 10 Disagree

13. I have a tendency to dominate conversations.
    Agree 1 2 3 4 5 6 7 8 9 10 Disagree

14. "Business meeting" should be the deciding and "planning hub" of the team.
    Agree 1 2 3 4 5 6 7 8 9 10 Disagree

15. All team members have equal authority.
    Agree 1 2 3 4 5 6 7 8 9 10 Disagree

16. I am a good listener.
    Agree 1 2 3 4 5 6 7 8 9 10 Disagree

17. Sometimes I may come across as offensively self-assured.
    Agree 1 2 3 4 5 6 7 8 9 10 Disagree

18. True leadership begins at "the top" and moves downward.
    Agree 1 2 3 4 5 6 7 8 9 10 Disagree

19. The entire team should have "final say" of any changes.
    Agree 1 2 3 4 5 6 7 8 9 10 Disagree

20. I like to work with people on an equal basis.
    Agree 1 2 3 4 5 6 7 8 9 10 Disagree

21. I have found myself exercising unwarranted influence over others.
    Agree 1 2 3 4 5 6 7 8 9 10 Disagree

22. Every team needs a clear "vertical chain of command."
    Agree 1 2 3 4 5 6 7 8 9 10 Disagree

23. No change in the team should be attempted without "majority" support.
    Agree 1 2 3 4 5 6 7 8 9 10 Disagree

24. I am tolerant with those I disagree with.
    Agree 1 2 3 4 5 6 7 8 9 10 Disagree

25. I believe "leaders" should not be questioned.
    Agree 1 2 3 4 5 6 7 8 9 10 Disagree

26. Every task in teamwork must follow a detailed procedure.
    Agree 1 2 3 4 5 6 7 8 9 10 Disagree

27. "Inactive" members have the same voting rights pertaining to decisions as "active" members.
    Agree 1 2 3 4 5 6 7 8 9 10 Disagree

28. I feel comfortable working with "groups of people."
    Agree 1 2 3 4 5 6 7 8 9 10 Disagree

29. I enjoy "flying solo."
    Agree 1 2 3 4 5 6 7 8 9 10 Disagree

30. Every team member must be accountable to a system of management.
    Agree 1 2 3 4 5 6 7 8 9 10 Disagree

31. No decision should be made without a thorough education of the entire team.
    Agree 1 2 3 4 5 6 7 8 9 10 Disagree

32. I am able to motivate others.

Agree 1 2 3 4 5 6 7 8 9 10 Disagree

After answering the questions to the **Leadership Questionnaire** take your score for answer 1 and place it beside the 1 in the chart below. Do this for each question. Then, total each column of questions and enter the score in the total below. What kind of leadership character are you?

Autocratic Leader	Bureaucrat Leader	Democratic Leader	Team Leader
1.	2.	3.	4.
5.	6.	7.	8.
9.	10.	11.	12.
13.	14.	15.	16.
17.	18.	19.	20.
21.	22.	23.	24.
25.	26.	27.	28.
29.	30.	31.	32.
Total	Total	Total	Total

What is your leadership style?

What Else Describes a Strong Leader?

If you could define a "strong leader" what would that person look like? Peter Druker explained leadership when he said, "Leadership is not magnetic personality, that can just as well be a glib tongue. It is not "making friends and influencing people", that

> A leader is someone who inspires others to see possibilities.

is flattery. Leadership is lifting a person's vision to higher sights, the raising of a person's performance to a higher standard, the building of a personality beyond its normal limitations." (Peter F. Drucker, *Management: Tasks, Responsibilities, Practices*) A leader is someone who inspires others to see possibilities. Here are fourteen characteristics of a strong leader that create and develop leadership in others.

1. A strong leader has qualities that cause people to follow them. Many people never find these qualities. The first step is to dig deep into ourselves to discover whom God has created us to be. A healthy leader is someone who draws people out of the crowd. Sam Walton once said, "Outstanding leaders go out of their way to boost the self-esteem of their personnel. If people believe in themselves, it is amazing what they can accomplish." Just about everyone is drawn to a leader who seeks out and promotes the best in a crowd.

2. A strong leader can inspire others to go beyond themselves. This can never happen until the leader goes first. It is impossible to help others see their potential until the one attempting to lead has a clear understanding of who they are! John Quincy Adams wrote, "If your actions inspire others to dream more, learn more, do more and become more, you are a leader."

3. A strong leader inspires trust. If those who follow you cannot trust you then, you will never be able to inspire them! Trust is necessary to grow the purpose and direction of any organization of people. Trust grows teamwork. King Solomon in the Old Testament had some positive words about working together when he wrote these words,
   "Two are better than one, because they have a good reward for their toil. For if they fall, one will lift up his fellow. But woe to him who is alone when he falls and has not another to lift him up! Again, if two lie together, they keep warm, but how can one keep warm alone? And

though a man might prevail against one who is alone, two will withstand him—a threefold cord is not quickly broken." (Ecclesiastes 4:9-12, ESV)

4. A strong leader has a consistent character. Strong leadership does not waver? There will be times when a leader will grow and change, but his or her character of honesty will never be questioned. Douglas MacArthur put it this way when he said, "A true leader has the confidence to stand alone, the courage to make tough decisions, and the compassion to listen to the needs of others. He does not set out to be a leader, but becomes one by the equality of his actions and the integrity of his intent."

5. A strong leader motivates by his or her words and actions. If the actions and behavior of leaders contradict their character and convictions, they will not be able to lead their team. If their behavior does not match their words, it will destroy any leadership influence.

6. A strong leader is not afraid of responsibility. A healthy leader is willing to hold his or her ground even when things get tough. Conflict and disagreement do not chase a true leader away.

7. A strong leader is willing to be accountable. When no one else is willing to take the blame, a true leader will step forward. Accountability is part of a true leader's character.

8. A strong leader does not fear the possibility of failure. In fact, true leaders brace themselves for such a possibility. They do not desire failure, but they understand that failure could happen when the diversities of individual people are brought together.

9. A strong leader does not blame others. A healthy leader does not point his finger at others when things get tough. Blaming other people for a flaw or mistake is not the character of a true leader.

10. A strong leader does not seek the reasons for failure in sources outside of himself or herself. A healthy leader is always looking for the reasons from within. "How should I have done this

differently?" "What would have been a better choice for me to make?" "Did I think this through?"

11. A strong leader inspires others to catch the vision! A good leader can help others own the vision and can help create ownership in such a way that others on the team feel they had created it.

12. A strong leader is endlessly evolving as a strong listener. Paying attention to ideas, visions, goals, hopes and dreams of others is the character of a good listener. A strong leader practices this behavior on a regular basis.

13. A strong leader always puts the needs of others above his own and understands that every member of the team is essential for that organization to be successful. Healthy leaders are constantly putting others ahead of themselves.

14. A strong leader is consistent in character, behavior and practices. A "wishy-washy" personality will destroy any leadership influence. Consistency in character is an absolute must for a leader to grow their influence.

Servant Leadership is the Goal of The Jethro Ministry

Real leaders understand servant leadership. In the past two decades leadership styles have changed tremendously. Top down leadership is dead! Those who work in various businesses, volunteer groups, charity organizations and congregations have come to believe that they should be involved in the decision making processes of their group. Those who are proving themselves to be productive and successful leaders have embraced the idea of merging with those they are attempting to lead. The business world also seems to have engaged the idea that it is better for a leader to encounter those they are attempting to lead on level ground.

> Those who are proving themselves to be productive and successful leaders have embraced the idea of merging with those they are attempting to lead.

In his article, *Effective Leadership Strategies for CEOs*, Ethan Lyon makes this point about top down leadership:

> "If a CEO meets their employees on the ground level and can show there is not a rigid hierarchical barrier between them and the rest of their company, word-of-mouth can spread to show they are not above, but with them" (*Effective Leadership Strategies for CEOs*, Ethan Lyon)

Top down leadership will not do very well any longer, however, a servant-leader can be very healthy for any organization. Someone who sees himself or herself as a servant rather than a dictator will find powerful principles in this mode of thinking. It was obvious that Jethro understood the servant leader role.

- A servant leader believes that his or her overall objective is to make the team feel successful.
- A servant leader does not see those in the organization as personal servants.
- A servant leader's main objective is to help accomplish the mission of the organization by encouraging every member of that organization.
- A servant leader understands that their main role is to be the "coach" of the team. Every good coach knows that for the team to be productive every member of that team must be encouraged and built up.

Jesus Christ set the best example of servant leadership known to humanity. His style of servant leadership was shown even up to the last supper he had with his disciples. As the disciples came in for the meal Jesus met them at the door as a servant would meet his master to wash the dirt from their feet. The Gospel of John, explains this event:

"Then He poured water into the basin, and began to wash the disciples' feet and to wipe them with the towel with which He was girded. So He came to Simon Peter. He said to Him, "Lord, do You wash my feet?" Jesus answered and said to him, "What I do you do not realize now, but you will understand hereafter." Peter said to Him, "Never shall You wash my feet!" Jesus answered him, "If I do not wash you, you have no part with Me." Simon Peter said to Him, "Lord, then wash not only my feet, but also my hands and my head." ....So when He had washed their feet, and taken His garments and reclined at the table again, He said to them, "Do you know what I have done to you? You call Me Teacher and Lord; and you are right, for so I am. If I then, the Lord and the Teacher, washed your feet, you also ought to wash one another's feet. For I gave you an example that you also should do as I did to you. Truly, truly, I say to you, a slave is not greater than his master, nor is one who is sent greater than the one who sent him." (John 13:5-16, NASB)

When defining servant leadership Hanz Finzel put it this way, "Here is the bottom line on servant leadership: The focus of a servant-leader is creating the best climate and investing in human cultivation, not majoring in control." (*Leaders on Leadership: Wisdom, Advice and Encouragement on the Art of Leading God's People,* page 274)

Jethro gave Moses some powerful advice on how to organize God's people on leading and serving. A key lesson that can be noticed in Jethro's conversation with Moses was the willingness of Moses to listen to the advice of a seasoned leader. A strong leader, like Moses, is easy to approach. They are willing to listen and they are also willing to change. Strong leadership grows out of this type of behavior.

8 ATTRIBUTES NEEDED FOR A HIGH-PERFORMANCE TEAM

8 Attributes Needed for a High-performance Team

■   ■   ■

Buchholz, Roth, and Hess in their book *Creating the High Performance Team* state that there are eight attributes evident in all high-performance teams. However it should be noted that even while examining these attributes, it is necessary to understand that many common problems affect the development of every team. Since teams are created by individuals seeking a common goal, the leader should recognize that the process is not much different from the development of a well-trained professional football team. Even well paid, professional, and skilled teams have problems. These types of problems can also be seen in a fellowship of believers who are trying to create a healthy ministry. Such problematic issues are:

- Some individuals never learn what their assignments are, particularly for certain plays or situations.
- Some are afraid of the coach, so they pretend to know things when they should be asking questions.
- Some want to do things "the old way," while others feel that more modern methods help.

- Factions and cliques quarrel and fight.
- The whole unit has not come together to develop common and committed goals.
- Decisions are made by someone, but some people either don't "get the word" or they disagree silently with the decision and drag their feet.
- Jealousy arises between people who then fail to work together.
- Even when people are aware of the problem, they do not know exactly what to do about it. (William Dyer, *Team Building* (Reading: Addison-Wesley Publishing Company 1987, page 4)

With these facts established, the eight attributes of high-performance teams can be grasped more clearly. The first attribute of a high-performance team is **participative leadership**. This leadership is the attribute that creates interdependence among team members and encourages an attitude of empowering, freeing up, and serving of others. (Steve Buchholz, Roth Thomas, Karen Hess, *Creating the High Performance Team*, New York: John Wiley and Sons, 1987, page 176) It is impossible for teams to function without the personal involvement of the team leader. This characteristic was what Jethro was encouraging Moses to develop when he told him that he needed help.

The second attribute is that of **shared responsibility**. The development of this trait is an attempt to instill in each team member the idea that the role they play is as important and valuable as those of the leaders of the team. (*Creating the High Performance Team*, page 176) The team demonstrates that there is value and respect for other team members when:

- They listen to each other's point of view.
- They do not become defensive with each other.
- They do not talk behind each other's back.
- They express their feelings with tact.
- They use persuasion instead of criticism.
- They praise each other for good individual and team effort.

- They do not blame each other or engage in scapegoating. (Edwin T. Cornelius, Involvement *Skills for Team Leaders and Supervisors,* Daniel Management Center, College of Business Administration, University of South Carolina, Columbia, S.C., page 3)

The third attribute of high-performance teams is **an understanding as to why the team has come together.** Having a sense of common purpose is evident in successful teams. Building a quality team requires the sharing of character traits. Those traits are:

1. Having a clear sense of purpose. Why are we a team? What are we trying to produce?
2. Having clear performance goals. What is our output? How will our performance be measured?
3. Understanding the value of a team that works together. How is the whole greater than the sum of the parts?
4. Having a sense of interdependence. What responsibilities do we have that produces a higher quality product? Where can the collective wisdom of the group outperform individual outputs?
5. Holding each other accountable for the output of the team. Are we willing to hold each other accountable not only for our individual contributions but also for the output of the team? (Jennifer M. Howard and Lawrence M. Miller, Team Management, Atlanta, The Miller Consultant Group, 1994, page 37)

Fourth, the high-performance team affords **a climate of clear and high communication.** A high-performance team creates an environment that produces trust and clear, honest communication. (*Creating the High Performance Team,* page 176)

> Leaders communicate in many ways. In fact, it is hard for them *not* to communicate, for they are so closely watched, referred to, and emulated that whatever they do or say - and even what they don't do or don't say - communicates

volumes to others. (Burt Nanus, *Visionary Leadership*, San Fraublishers: Jossey- Bass Publishers, 1992, page 136)

Fifth, the high-performance team **is not threatened by change and growth**. In fact, an efficient team sees a changing future as an opportunity for growth and expansion. Miller says, "The behavior of leaders, the course they steer, the confidence they inspire, will do more to influence change than all the tools and techniques." (Lawrence Miller, *Design for Total Quality: A Workbook for Socio-Technical Design*, Atlanta: The Millers Consulting Group, Inc. 1991, page 29)

The sixth attribute of high-performance teams is **keeping a clear focus on the task at hand**. Meetings, as well as the organization of the group, keep their focus upon the ultimate goal. (*Creating High Performance Teams*, page 177) Communication works best when shared in a personal nature.

Seventh, a high-performance team **maximizes the talents of the team members**. The leaders remove any barriers that would hinder the use of gifts or talents. The use of skills by the individual are maximized and encouraged.

The eighth attribute of high-performance teams is that of **practicing a rapid response**. Good response is the skill of an organization to identify an opportunity and to act upon it quickly. It is the skill of working in harmony at a quick pace.

For *The Jethro Ministry* to work well the eight attributes in this chapter need to be part of the ministry structure:

1. Participative leadership
2. Shared responsibility
3. Understanding why the team has been brought together
4. Clear and high communication
5. Not threatened by change and growth
6. Keeping a clear focus on the task at hand
7. Maximizing the talents of the team members
8. Practicing rapid responses

Encouraging people to work together is a challenge. According to Max Depree, leading a team of different individuals with various talents is like leading a jazz band:

> "Jazz-band leaders must choose the music, find the right musicians, and perform in public. But the effect of the performance depends on so many things – the environment, the volunteers playing the band, the need for everybody to perform as individuals and as a group, the absolute dependence of the leader on the members of the band, the need of the leader for the followers to play well." (Max Depree, *Leadership Jazz*, New York; Doubleday, 1992, pages 8-9)

Depree's approach and analogy are extremely healthy. The team cannot perform to its maximum abilities without each member of the team (band) taking part. For any team to be successful, there must be an absolute dependency of the leader on the members of the band. For team development to take place within the local church, the pastor must become comfortable with the concept that he cannot play all the instruments that are needed to create a successful ministry. The pastor may have the ability to play many roles, but for the church to work at its maximum potential the encouragement and empowerment of others is essential. The goal is for every team member to use those abilities and gifts that God has given them in their individual uniqueness. The process that creates a healthy and successful team grows upon the leader's desire to see such a creation take place. A high-performance and well-organized team is what Jethro was leading Moses to see in Exodus 18.

HEALTHY LEADERSHIP FOR A NEW CENTURY

Healthy Leadership for
a New Century

■ ■ ■

In the past one hundred years, the church has placed upon its leaders more responsibility than ever before. In a recent conference, I took a class on time management only to be thoroughly discouraged by the speaker that day. The leader of the conference told us with great pride how he worked sixty plus hours a week. His goal was to instruct us how to do the same by adequate time management. I must confess that this was an extremely frustrating two hours for me. I had no desire to put more on my plate than I already had, nor was I aiming to become proud of an addiction to work.

The result of too much work on too few people is one of the most destructive tools that Satan employs today. Many years ago while pastoring in North Carolina, I witnessed an epidemic of ministry burnout the like of which I had never seen before and never hope to see again. The congregations and ministries involved had several common themes:

1. All the churches placed a great deal of responsibility upon the pastor as being **the** primary caregiver for the congregation. This

behavior seemed to work well as long as the congregations had an attendance of fewer than one hundred people.

2. The role of the deacons in these churches was that of "administrators" not "ministers." Needs of the budget, construction, taking care of the property, and many other tasks took priority over the needs of the people.

3. All the pastors were sincere, hard working men who found themselves caught in a web of church responsibilities, family loyalties, and not enough time in a day. These life demands became an area of personal conflict for some of the pastors.

4. As the churches grew, the mechanisms to "take care" of those coming into the churches did not change. These demands were similar to the situation where Jethro found Moses working. It was a situation of one man trying to take care of the many.

5. Most of these churches were rural churches that were feeling the sprawl of a growing metro area. The country farms were becoming suburbs. The adjustments for the congregations were not easy in most cases. These changes led to more stress for all involved.

6. The pastors in these churches were being called upon to be more than their training had prepared them to be. In the past century, the local pastor has become counselor, advisor, politician, preacher, evangelist, teacher, caregiver, technical adviser, educational director, C.E.O and much more depending upon the expectations of the congregation.

What Does a Healthy and Effective Leader Look Like?

We all are leaders at some time in our lives. Decisions will be made that will lead us to blaze a trail that others will follow. This may take place among our friends, as a parent, as a volunteer, as a business person or as a leader within our congregation. What makes a true leader? How does someone know when he or she is being a strong and productive leader?

There have been many seminars, training courses, and books written about leadership. But how does someone know if they are showing signs and talents of a healthy leader? Here are 9 principles of a healthy leader to consider.

1. Healthy Leaders Accept Responsibility

In any organization, someone is going to have to take responsibility. A healthy leader is willing to take on the responsibility. Even though it may require many hours and a lot of dedication, this person is willing to do it. Responsibility does not produce fear in this type of individual. Responsibility for the healthy leader opens his or her eyes to possibilities.

2. Healthy Leaders Do Not Have a Problem in the Delegation of Responsibility

A healthy leader is constantly looking for the skills and talents of other people. This is what Jethro told Moses he had to do. This leader understands that their abilities are limited. Discovering the gifts and skills of other people is top on the list for this leader. This individual understands that the combined resources of diverse personalities are powerful.

> A healthy leader is constantly looking for the skills and talents of other people. This is what Jethro told Moses he had to do.

3. Healthy Leaders are Influencers

A healthy leader is constantly encouraging others to discover their own abilities and gifts. You will never find this leader coming across in negative tones. In fact, those who have the ability of strong leadership are pleasant to be around. In Exodus 18, the reader will never sense that Moses felt he was being criticized by Jethro. Healthy leaders are extremely positive. They are example setters. Albert Schweitzer once said, "Example is not the main thing in influencing others. It is the only thing."

Our healthy influence as leaders on individual people runs deep and wide. John Maxwell said, "Leadership is not about titles, positions or flowcharts. It is about one life influencing another."

4. Healthy Leaders Understand the Role They Play in the Lives of Others

Someone who has the ability to be an influential leader understands the role they play in the lives of people. The value of the individual ranks high on the list of most important things to a true leader. They understand that their words and their attitude will create or destroy strong teamwork. The individual is the most important resource to the healthy leader. The business, the organization, and even money do not mean as much to the true leader as the person they have been called to lead. What a leader says, what a leader does, will be a determining factor whether someone wants to be part of the organization or not.

> The individual is the most important resource to the healthy leader.

5. Healthy Leaders Aim to Influence Those Around Them

Healthy leaders are not dictators. Healthy leaders are not bosses. Healthy leaders are not overwhelming personalities that aim to have the upper hand. The goal of this team leader is to evolve into becoming an influencer.

6. Healthy Leaders Are Always in the Process of Learning

One becomes a healthy leader by constantly being involved in learning. This learning takes place wherever and whenever it can be engaged. This type of leadership personality never gets to a point in their life at which they feel they have accomplished it all. A healthy leader is a seeker. Learning leaders are on a constant treasure hunt. Even when they find a great treasure, they will soon be looking for a better discovery.

7. Healthy Leaders are Great Communicators

Someone who is seeking to be a productive leader will also be someone who works hard in the development of his or her communications skills. The ability to communicate one-on-one is a true skill of a healthy leader. Speaking to a large gathering is impressive; however, the healthy leader

> The ability to communicate one-on-one is a true skill of a healthy leader.

is always looking for the opportunity to spend time with people in a personal fashion. In his training and coaching of the disciples, Jesus was often pulling the disciples away from the crowds to spend time with them in a smaller gathering.

8. Healthy Leaders Understand That They Are Not Self-made

Pride and arrogance are not characteristics of a healthy leader. This individual understands that the reason that they have the abilities they do is because they have learned the skills from someone else. They are not self-made, and they know it. In fact, this personality would never make a claim of being self-made.

9. Healthy Leaders are Always in the Process of Learning

For a healthy leader learning never stops. It never ceases. It goes on and on, and they are never bored with it. John F. Kennedy once said, "Leadership and learning are indispensable to each other." You cannot separate a healthy leader from constant learning. Those who have the skills of healthy leadership see it as a growing process. When one becomes a healthy leader, he or she also becomes an effective leader.

Healthy Leaders Grow Into Effective Leaders

Effective leadership has certain basic visionary characteristics. The aim of strong leaders is to translate their "vision" into reality. So, how is this done? Here are 12 characteristics of an effective leader to consider.

1. An Effective Leader is a Risk-Taker

Effective leaders attempt to bring about great changes. These changes are not without risks. Facing changes and challenges, as we get older is a part of life. How we deal with changes and challenges reflects on who we are and how we will grow as a leader.

A strong leader is very creative. They will try new approaches even if it presents possible failure. Effective leaders recognize that failure is only temporary and that this setback gives a clearer understanding of what not to do in the future. The overall attitude of a risk-taking leader is, "You ultimately fail when you do not give it a try!"

Helen Keller was born in 1882. She became ill as a young child and was struck blind, deaf and mute. In 1887, Keller had a teacher named Anne Sullivan who helped her make tremendous progress in her ability to communicate. As she grew up under Sullivan's coaching she went on to college, graduating in 1904. One of Keller's famous quotes showed her as a risk-taker. She said, "Life is either a daring adventure or nothing at all."

2. An Effective Leader has Self-control

Strong leaders know that their ability to stay calm, even in the worst of conflicts, is a character trait that must be nurtured and grown. The effective leader's mantra is, "When you lose your temper, you lose."

Stephen Covey pointed out that there is a well-defined character of those who express self-control. He said, "You have to decide what your highest priorities are and have the courage - pleasantly, smilingly, non-apologetically - to say 'no' to other things. And the way to do that is by having a bigger 'yes' burning inside. The enemy of the 'best' is often the 'good.'" Self-control will determine what is most important.

3. An Effective Leader is a Caring Individual

Strong leadership can never take place if those we lead think we do not care. Leaders should show a caring attitude about the mission of their organization; however, their concern for each team member must take priority over everything else.

> Leaders should show a caring attitude about the mission of their organization; however, their concern for each team member must take priority over everything else.

When a leader cares about those they lead, they show behavior that is consistently acknowledging others. A leader who cares is also one who maintains eye contact during a conversation. This leader asks many questions and listens more than they talk. A caring leader desires the feedback and opinions of those they lead. Jethro and Jesus both asked questions of those they were attempting to lead.

Due to their caring nature, leaders regularly compliment people in public and private settings. Leaders of this type also express genuine interest in the lives of those they lead.

4. An Effective Leader is Modest

Self-evaluation is a strong characteristic of an effective leader. A good leader does not have a problem in being evaluated or receiving criticism. No one enjoys being corrected, but an effective leader sees it for what it is: an opportunity for personal growth.

5. An Effective Leader is Balanced

Good leaders do not ignore any area of their personal lives. They understand that to do well they must keep up good health, physically, spiritually, emotionally and mentally.

An effective leader understands that to be a balanced leader it is necessary to:

1. Rest, and get enough sleep
2. Eat a healthy diet
3. Exercise on a regular basis
4. Work hard on developing healthy social skills and interaction
5. Grow personal skills and talents

The overriding goal of a strong leader is to go at all areas of life in a balanced fashion.

6. An Effective Leader is Resolute

Strong leaders must make wise decisions and must be willing to listen to wise counsel. A strong leader is determined and admirably purposeful. There is a strong character of unwavering determination. The word resolute describes a characteristic of firmness and determination. A strong leader is clear in purpose and belief. A resolute leader can also be characterized by quickness.

7. An Effective Leader is Motivational

Motivational leaders enjoy their task. They are optimistic about their purpose. Change requires taking risks, personal growth and challenges. A motivational leader does not back down from a challenge but is willing to lead the way as an inspirational leader.

8. An Effective Leader is a Clear Communicator

> The skill of communication is grown upon the skill of listening.

It is important to understand that communication is not solely conversation. A good communicator aims to make sure that his or her message is understood. The skill of communication is grown upon the skill of listening. Listening is as important as talking, and an effective leader listens more than he or she talks.

9. An Effective Leader is a Visionary

A leader must be a dreamer. A productive leader is someone who can see into the future. The challenge for every visionary leader is not to get so far ahead of the team in what they see that they leave them behind, lost, wandering about the future direction. A visionary is not only a dreamer but also a strong communicator of the dream.

Effective leadership has certain, basic, visionary, characteristics. The aim of a strong leader is to translate their "vision" into reality.

10. An Effective Leader has a Sense of Humor

Good leaders take their work seriously; however, they do not mind laughing at themselves. Healthy leaders do not have a problem in finding humor in their mistakes or blunders. A productive leader knows that laughter is good for the soul. A humorous person can lead a team even through the most challenging times.

Dwight D. Eisenhower said, "A sense of humor is part of the art of leadership, of getting along with people, of getting things done." William Arthur Ward put it this way, "A well-developed sense of humor is the pole that adds balance to your steps as you walk the tightrope of life."

11. An Effective Leader is Ethical

A strong leader has a strong moral base. There is no question about the leader's character. What you see is what you get. There is nothing more defeatist than a dishonest or lying leader. A strong leader has strong convictions. Ethical living and leadership will take courage and conviction. It means doing the right thing, even when the right

> Ethical living and leadership will take courage and conviction. It means doing the right thing, even when the right thing is not popular or easy to accomplish.

thing is not popular or easy to accomplish. When a leader makes decisions based on core values, then it makes a clear statement that this leader cannot be bought. The effective, ethical leader leads by example.

12. An Effective Leader is Dedicated to the "Cause"

Being an effective leader is not easy but it is necessary for the success of any organization or team. Dedication is key. Being able to convey a commitment to a clear purpose and cause is essential. The strong leader will communicate the "cause" as often as possible.

Real dedication is fueled by the passion of the cause. If there is no passion, then there is no motivation for the cause. This applies to the purpose and the cause of *The Jethro Ministry*.

Every successful team needs a healthy and effective leader! The goal of all leaders should be to ask a simple question of themselves, "Am I being a healthy and effective leader?" Asking questions was a basic practice of the teaching style of Moses' father-in-law. Jethro asked Moses to consider what he was trying to be when he asked, "Why are you doing what you are doing?" (Exodus 18:14)) The ability to personally know who we are and our leadership character is key to the success of *The Jethro Ministry*.

WHAT ABOUT THE BOARD OF DEACONS?

What About The Board of Deacons?

■　■　■

Many churches claim that they are "people of the Book (the Bible)." I have always found this to be encouraging. At the same time, it is also somewhat amazing that the very people who claim to be "people of the Book" are also those who use a phrase that has no biblical foundation to describe one of the most active ministry teams in the church: Board of deacons! The term "board of deacons" cannot be found in the Bible. "Deacon" can be found but "board of" is completely and totally absent. The word deacon or *diakonos* (Greek) means "servant, attendant, minister." ("Deacon", *The Interpreters Dictionary of the Bible,* Abingdon Press; Nashville, 1962, page 785) Where did the phrase "board of deacons" come from? From all indications, it appears that the term was created during the industrial age to describe those who sat around a table, or board, to make decisions for the company.

> The term "board of deacons" cannot be found in the Bible. "Deacon" can be found but "board of" is completely and totally absent.

First of all, the church is not a company. Secondly, deacons have been called to *serve*, not meet around a table and make decisions for the masses. *The Jethro Ministry* is for deacons who wish to serve and churches that wish to follow the guidance of the Bible. It is for congregations who are willing to grow in service. With these thoughts in mind there are certain facts you should know about *The Jethro Ministry*:

1. This ministry will not appeal to every congregation. Not because it is not correct and Biblically based but because "tradition" has a stronger hold on some fellowships than scripture does.
2. This ministry is for pastors and church leaders who are willing to lead the church by the word of God rather than by traditions.
3. This ministry is an attempt to respect, preserve, and love those who help lead.
4. *The Jethro Ministry* is an attempt to draw the congregation together as a ministry team.
5. *The Jethro Ministry* is an attempt to stay true to the word of God in caring for the people of God.

The relationships leaders have with the deacons of the church are key in evaluating the condition of any congregation. The pastor needs the deacons and the deacons need pastoral leadership. The roles of these two groups vary from church to church. There are denominations that have both elders and deacons, and there are others that have only deacons. The situation of those congregations without elders usually requires the deacons to carry the responsibility of maintenance and ministry within the local congregation. These tasks are overwhelming and somewhat impossible for most deacons.

The Jethro Ministry recognizes that the ministry to the congregation is the priority of the deacons. One of the first challenges that *The Jethro Ministry* puts before the congregation is that of changing what has become decades of tradition regarding the work of deacons in the congregation. Care for the people of God is not a fad or a new idea. Caring comes from the word of God beginning in the Old Testament and carrying over into the ministry of Jesus in the New Testament and the early church as demonstrated in the book of Acts (Acts 6, NASB). The church does its best when its total ministry is based upon scripture. The world has many good ideas and approaches to ministry, but the word of God is that which gives a solid foundation. The writer of Proverbs says,

> "Every word of God is flawless; he is a shield to those who
> take refuge in him." (Proverbs 30:5, NIV)

Jesus said on one occasion that there were those who claimed to be followers of God, yet "nullify the word of God for the sake of your traditions." (Matthew 15:6, NIV) There is that word again, "tradition". So, what does the scripture say deacons are called to be? The Apostle Paul gave ten guidelines for choosing deacons in the church. Paul writes to Timothy (I Timothy 3:8-13, NASB) that deacons should:

- Be men of dignity
- Not be double-tongued
- Not be addicted to much wine
- Not be greedy for money
- Hold to the mystery of the faith
- Have a clear conscience
- Be tested
- Be beyond reproach
- Be the husband of only one wife
- Be good managers of their children and their own households

Diakonos has several meanings. It can be translated as "one who renders service to another." It also means "attendant" or "servant." There are also times when deacon is translated to refer to one who "executes a commission." However, *diakonos* is not always translated as deacon. When Jesus used the word *diakonos,* He used it to refer to the service in the Kingdom of God. Jesus' advice to those who desired to lead was to take on the role of a servant (*diakonos*).

"It is not this way among you, but whoever wishes to become great among you shall be your servant, and whoever wishes to be first among you shall be your slave;" (Matthew 20-26-27, NASB)

A deacon is someone who is under the authority and leadership of someone else. The objective is to serve. Jesus had much to say about service and those who serve:

"Be like men who are waiting for their master when he returns from the wedding feast, so that they may immediately open *the door* to him when he comes and knocks. Blessed are those slaves whom the master will find on the alert when he comes; truly I say to you, that he will gird himself *to serve*, and have them recline *at the table*, and will come up and wait on them." (Luke 12:36-37, NASB)

Jesus calls his servants to be ready to serve. Service is the main objective. The goal of a true servant of God is to be sure the needs of others are met before their own. Jesus promotes an attitude of total service to others. He said to his disciples,

"And He said to them, "The kings of the Gentiles lord it over them; and those who have authority over them are called 'Benefactors.' But *it is* not this way with you, but the one who is the greatest among you must become like the youngest, and the leader like the servant. For who is greater, the one who reclines *at the table* or the one who serves? Is it not the one who reclines *at the table*? But I am among you as the one who serves. (Luke 22:25-27, NASB)

According to Jesus, the perfect servant has two outstanding traits. They could be first, but they position themselves last. Likewise, they could command but are willing to take orders. Jesus makes a promise to those who are willing to be His servants. "If anyone serves Me, he must follow Me; and where I am, there My servant will be also; if anyone serves Me, the Father will honor him." (John 12:26, NASB) This can apply to the deacons of any congregation.

> Jesus taught that greatness is found in service to others. Jesus told his disciples that "the greatest among you shall be your servant."

In a study of scripture, there are three basic principles which Jesus taught relating to servanthood. First, Jesus taught that greatness is found in service to others. Jesus told his disciples that "the greatest among you shall be your servant." (Matthew 23:11, NASB) This is not the desire of a worldly mind. This is the call of the Lord Jesus to all His followers.

The second principle of servanthood is that the aim of the true servant of Christ is to allow the needs, cares, and burdens of others to take first place.

> "And sitting down, He called the twelve and said to them, "If anyone wants to be first, he shall be last of all, and servant of all." (Mark 9:35, NASB)

The example of Christ sets the third principle. Jesus came to serve not to be served. He calls his followers to the same.

> "But Jesus called them to Himself, and said, "You know that the rulers of the Gentiles lord it over them, and *their* great men exercise authority over them. "It is not so among you, but whoever wishes to become great among you shall be your servant, and whoever wishes to be first among you shall be your slave; just as the Son of Man did not come to be served, but to serve, and to give His life a ransom for many." (Matthew 20:25-28, NASB)

Compare the words of Jesus and Paul as they both refer to service.

Jesus	Paul
"His master said to him, 'Well done, good and faithful *slave;* you were faithful with a few things, I will put you in charge of many things, enter into the joy of your master." (Matthew 25:21, NASB)	"For those who have served well as *deacons* obtain for themselves a high standing and great confidence in the faith that is in Christ Jesus." (I Timothy 3:13, NASB)

There is a great paradox in these passages of scripture. They both teach that servants are the greatest people in the Kingdom of God. This goes against the standards and norms of the world. In fact, this goes against the standards and principles of most people within and without the church. This is why the advice of Paul in I Timothy 5:22 should be heeded. Don't choose a deacon (servant) in a hurry! Servanthood does not come easy in a world that is self-serving. In fact, the world sees the concept of Christian service as something odd and to be avoided. *The Jethro Ministry* is all about servanthood and the deacons are called to show this example of the church to the world.

BEHAVIORS THAT CAN DESTROY THE JETHRO MINISTRY BEFORE IT STARTS

Behaviors That Can Destroy The Jethro Ministry Before It Starts

■   ■   ■

The Old Testament Ignored in Ministry Development

For over a year while I was in college I attended a church in which the pastor never preached a message from the Old Testament. The Old Testament was never used to teach his congregation the plan and directions of God. I have in my ministry come across several pastors who have a reluctance to use the Old Testament. The stories are unfamiliar to many of our members and the truths they teach are being ignored. I have had more than one person respond when I mention *"The Jethro Ministry"* by making a comical comment about Jethro on an old sitcom "The Beverly Hillbillies" that ran from 1962 to 1971. I am sure this was meant as a humorous remark; however, I am also sure that there are probably a great many church members who know more about Jethro, the hillbilly, than they do about Jethro, the priest of Midian.

When Jesus experienced temptation in the wilderness, he taught us about how he regarded the Old Testament. On every occasion that

Satan came and tempted him the Lord responded with Old Testament scripture. When tempted Jesus used scripture from Deuteronomy 8:3, Deuteronomy 6:16, and Deuteronomy 6:13, 10:20. The Lord set the example of using the Old Testament texts as His weapon in confronting the attacks of Satan. If Jesus used the Old Testament as foundational for His ministry, it would be extremely wise for us to follow His example. The examples of the Lord, as much as the Lord's words, are guidelines for the believer and the church. When challenged in his ministry, the Lord used the word of the Old Testament. In developing the ministry strategy of the church, it would be of great benefit to pay close attention to the guidance of the Old Testament scripture. Practicing this is especially true when dealing with a ministry that involves numbers of people. Thus, any congregation should not ignore the guidance of Exodus 18.

Traditions In the Church

Growing up in the south and immersed in the traditions of southern living introduced to me a treasury of truth. Church life was an important part of my early years. My first memories are fond ones that involved "dinner on the grounds" and "gospel music." Growing up in a pastor's home exposed me to varied environments at an early age. It brought me in contact with different people and cultures while my father attended seminary in New Orleans, and that broadened my perception of the world. From being taught the French language in the third grade to dining in the captain's galley on a Pakistani ship harbored on the Mississippi River, my early years were canvassed with the diversity of humanity. In all these adventures, the church has always been a part of my life. I have the utmost respect for those who have dedicated their time and efforts to the ministry of local congregations, and I value the traditions passed on to me. Traditions introduce a wealth of information and diversity of wisdom into our lives. Webster's dictionary says that "traditions" are:

> "an inherited, established, or customary pat-
> tern of thought or action: the handing down of

beliefs and customs by word of mouth or by example."
("Tradition" - *Webster' Dictionary*, Merriam-Webster,
Incorporated, Publishers; Massachusetts, 1995)

Traditions are healthy for stability in all our lives. Traditions can also be a death sentence to a Christian congregation if they become more important than the direction of the Lord. There are some congregations where traditions mean more to their fellowship than the moving and direction of the Holy Spirit. Jesus had some warnings concerning traditions.

> "You have let go of the commands of God and are holding on to human traditions. And he continued, "You have a fine way of setting aside the commands of God in order to observe your own traditions! (Mark 7:8-9, NIV)

The deacon/elder ministry of the congregation is probably one of the strongest traditions any fellowship has in place. To challenge this ministry or to suggest an alternative cuts at the very heart of many congregations. The focus of *The Jethro Ministry* is to take the church back to its roots. The goal is to seek the Holy Spirit and let Him direct the leaders of the church to become what scripture calls the church to be, rather than following the traditions of men.

The Misuse of Time

One of the greatest challenges the church has today is to recognize the demands on the fellowship. Churches have implemented many plans and ministries in order to care for church members as well as effectively reach the unchurched. Usually, these plans will take off and last until it is obvious that they are not productive. The immediate response from some would be, "You just don't have the right people helping you." Testimonies to this effect can be heard from churches large and small. It has nothing to do with the right people; it has a great deal to do with leading people in the right way. The work of the Kingdom is not easy and can be very taxing. There are elements in Kingdom work that Jesus explains when He says to His disciples:

> "Take my yoke upon you and learn from me, for I am gentle and humble in heart, and you will find rest for your souls. For my yoke is easy and my burden is light." (Matthew 11:29-30, NASB)

The ministry Jesus taught was a shared ministry. Jesus and his disciples had time for one another. The stress of present day ministry would be foreign to the early disciples, yet the total sacrifice of these disciples is foreign to many Christians today. There were moments of stress, yet there was a greater peace that enabled the apostles to fulfill the call of Christ. Even the Apostle Paul had a sense of peace in times of difficulty. While in jail awaiting his execution Paul was able to write words of encouragement to the church at Philippi:

> "Rejoice in the Lord always. I will say it again: Rejoice! Let your gentleness be evident to all. The Lord is near. Do not be anxious about anything, but in everything, by prayer and petition, with thanksgiving, present your requests to God. And the peace of God, which transcends all understanding, will guard your hearts and your minds in Christ Jesus." (Philippians 4:4-7, NIV)

Christian service should bring joy and peace to the follower of Christ. This type of service is odd to the modern mind. There are many who work endless hours and never receive what Paul was talking about. Work based upon a worldly approach does not produce what Paul taught the early Christians. If we desire to receive peace and satisfaction in our service, it must be based upon the word of God. This will lead to a healthy use of our personal time.

Unhealthy Work Habits

In 1998 Immanuel Baptist, a fellowship I pastored from 1996-2006, began a ministry dealing with those addicted to gambling. I discovered something through this ministry. There are many forms of addiction in the world. "Working" is for many people an addiction. Work addiction even includes church work. The inability to stop working, take a rest, and relax is as difficult for many people as trying to stop drinking, taking drugs or gambling. In fact, there are many who receive a "rush" from working to the point of exhaustion. This rush happens more often within the structure of church ministry than we may be willing to admit. The first paid position I had as a minister was not long after my eighteenth birthday. I remember the position with fondness, yet I also recall the endless hours I spent at the church. There would be some weeks in which I would be at the church every evening including Saturday and Sunday. It was difficult and intense work even for a teenager. I understand that the Lord expects our best, but I have come to believe that our best is not self-destructive. *The Jethro Ministry* is nothing new. Burnout from church work is nothing new. The teaching of Exodus 18 is the guidance given to Moses by a wise man. If one listens carefully to Jethro, one will benefit from seasoned wisdom. The pastor will survive; the deacons will have help, and the congregation will enter a spirit-filled time of ministry.

Ignoring the Small Group Strategy of Jesus

Many times we fail to see the obvious. There are many attempts to create new and exciting ways to minister and reach the world for Jesus while ignoring the simplest and most productive examples. When Jesus led His disciples, He led them with a simple and basic nature that could be understood by children. The parables that Jesus conveyed were truths that the young and old alike could embrace. One of the lessons that Jesus taught in His ministry is one which the church often ignores and in many cases refuses to embrace. To put it bluntly, Jesus did not seem to be impressed with the crowd. In fact, the Scripture records the Lord trying to escape to "a quiet place."

> "The apostles gathered around Jesus and reported to him all they had done and taught. Then, because so many people were coming and going that they did not even have a chance to eat, he said to them, "Come with me by yourselves to a quiet place and get some rest." (Mark 6:30-31, NIV)

Jesus' ministry with the twelve was an example of small group ministry. Jesus also had within the twelve a cluster of three: Simon Peter, James, and John. Never do we find the Lord setting an agenda for teaching the masses as He did the twelve. It is true that Jesus did teach large groups of people, yet His strategy in teaching the twelve cannot be overlooked.

The ministry of Jesus started by recruiting disciples to be a part of his team. It was clear from the beginning that Jesus had no intention of trying to do ministry alone. The strategy that Jesus used was one of training and deploying those he trained to go into the world. The three years of Jesus' ministry were spent equipping others for the task of continuing His work after his ascension.

Believing the Myth of "Knowing Everyone"

"I don't want our church to grow so large that I can't know everyone." How many times have God's people made this comment? This statement is made by people on opposite ends of the spectrum. On one end, you have a church member who truly would like to know every person who comes into the fellowship. These are personal, caring, people who allow their personality trait to limit the growth of the church due to their inability to "know" everyone. It is hard for the first group to see the church grow because they simply cannot "keep up". On the other end are those who have a degree of insecurity in allowing outsiders or new people into the workings of the fellowship. It is hard for the second group to see the

church grow because they simply cannot "keep" the church under their control.

The days of knowing everyone in the neighborhood are gone. This is a truth that many Americans have known for some time. However, this reality is a new realization for some people. It is a common event to watch moving vans proceeding in and out of any given neighborhood on any day of the week. This may sound depressing, but it could lead to one of the greatest ages for the church yet. Our neighborhoods are not what they once were, but our churches can become communities of faith like never before seen in the history of Christianity. In a recent conversation with one of the older members in a local church, I was told of days gone by. A time when everyone on the "mill hill" knew each other, worked together, raised children together, and went to church together. Now many of those same people do not know the people living two doors down from their home. I say this not to depress anyone but simply to describe the reality in which we find ourselves in the modern world.

The myth of knowing everyone is one that is hindering the work of the Kingdom of God. There are congregations that have designed their fellowships to stop growing by allowing this myth to be part of the development of their ministry. If there are more than fifteen families in your present fellowship, chances are you do not *know* them all. As you think upon this statement do not forget to include their children. Children count also. How well do you know those young souls? The ability for humans to make good friends is somewhat limited. To make friends requires time, dedication, and desire.

Worshipping with people on Sunday morning does not mean that you have had a personal encounter with that person; after all, the purpose of worship is to meet the Lord. There are many people who spend time with each other who do not know each other nor care for their company. There will be many people who go to church next Sunday and the idea of talking to everyone who is there does not cross their mind. Some of these same people will voice freely how they feel "our church is getting too large, I just don't know everybody anymore." I am not sure where we developed the notion that we are supposed to "know everyone" who attends our fellowship, but this notion is a real one.

Jesus took twelve men to teach and spend time with, not 120, not 1,200, and not 12,000. This was an amazing and interesting behavior of the Lord. If Jesus, being the Son of God and having all the attributes and character of His Father took only twelve men at a time, we are amiss if we do not follow His leadership in working in His church. It is a known fact that Jesus used this small group of men to change the world.

The way in which Jesus recruited and taught these men was uniquely powerful. The disciples were not consumed with what some followers of Jesus are consumed with today. They knew nothing of the production line. The men taught by Jesus had no understanding of mass production. Success for the disciples was seeing the conversion of an individual centurion or a tax collector. Jesus and His disciples worked on what some would call today a small scale.

The Jethro Ministry is a ministry that focuses upon the worth of the individual. Jethro gave Moses guidance concerning how to value the one over the many while at the same time taking care of the many. The next three chapters will take Exodus 18 and explain the strategy and a plan for developing *The Jethro Ministry* within any congregation.

THE TEAM MINISTRY OF JETHRO EXODUS 18

The Team Ministry of
Jethro: Exodus 18

■   ■   ■

xodus 18 is a story that outlines how to develop a team approach to
ministry. The story begins with Jethro, the priest of Midian, being
reunited with Moses, his son-in-law, in the desert. When Jethro hears of
all the successes of Moses, he is supportive of and positive towards Moses'
efforts. The old man rejoices at the great accomplishments of Moses. His
response is fourfold: First, Jethro rejoices "for all the good which the
Lord has done to Israel" (v.9). Second, he blesses Yahweh (v. 10). Third,
he makes a confession that, "Now I know that the Lord is greater than all
gods" (v. 11). Finally, he offers a burnt offering and sacrifices to God (v.
12) (Lester Meyer, *Message of Exodus*, Minneapolis: Publishing House,
1983, page 109).

The verb used in this passage of scripture for "rejoiced" is a Hebrew
word that is rarely used in the Old Testament. The translation gives the
impression that Jethro was "astonished" or "amazed" at all the good work
that was taking place under Moses' leadership. (J. Phillip Hyatt, *New
Century Bible Commentary: Exodus* Grand Rapids: Wm. B. Eerdmans
Publishing Company, 1971, page 189). There can be little doubt that

Moses was successful. Jethro was impressed by the accomplishments of Moses, but the wisdom of the seasoned priest was insightful. He observed problems with Moses' system of leadership, yet his first act was to compliment Moses on all the good he was accomplishing.

Encouragement is a sign of Jethro's healthy leadership style, but he was appalled at the inefficient teamwork with which Moses was attempting to minister to the people of God. The thoughts of Jethro are made obvious by the statements, "What you are doing is not good. You and these people who come to you will only wear yourselves out. The work is too heavy for you; you cannot handle it alone (Ex. 18:17-18, NIV)." Jethro saw the present conditions that Moses was working under as debilitating and knew what was about to take place. Moses would not be able to withstand the consistent and unyielding demand upon his life.

Jethro informed Moses that he was not doing well in his administration and delegation of the responsibilities of leadership. He also enlightened Moses to the fact that he would wear himself out (Exodus 18:18). The words used here which are translated as "to wear himself out" mean "to wither and fade away as a leaf." (F. B. Huey Jr., *Exodus*, Grand Rapids: Zondervan, 1977, page 77). The stresses were great upon Moses; however, Jethro had a plan. He informed Moses that if he would follow this plan he could survive and continue his ministry to God's people. The seasoned priest went on to inform Moses that he should not implement this plan unless he received the direction of God to do so (Ex 18:23).

Another perspective views the story of Jethro and his advice to Moses as a return of a favor. In Exodus 2:16-20 Moses came to Jethro during a time of crisis. Moses helped his future father-in-law in driving away shepherds of local tribes from his water well. It is now Jethro's turn to come and assist his son-in-law. Both incidents are accompanied by a meal and acts of kindness that result in making "shepherding" more effective. For Jethro, it helped in the shepherding of the flock; for Moses, it taught him how to shepherd God's people as they headed toward the Promise Land.

Jethro's guidance was strong and wise. Moses was dealing with thousands of people. The demands upon his time, and physical strength was exhausting. Jethro's plan involved two key elements: the delegation and division of responsibilities. The organizational plan that Jethro presented meant that Moses would delegate authority to key leaders. This organizational plan would mean that every potential leader would be given a place of key leadership. The delegation of ministry responsibilities would enable Moses to rest and plan for other responsibilities. Such a strategy of ministry would enable him to have time for other matters. One of the newest responsibilities Moses dealt with was the reunion of his family. The strategy of Jethro would allow Moses to have quality time to spend with his wife and children.

The ministry strategy that Jethro suggested is one that can be applicable for ministers today. The revealing of who God is and his designs for ministry comes in moments of divine revelation, yet God also uses those around us to reveal His will. The design and plan of Jethro's ministry emerged from the sound judgment of an experienced counselor. Jethro's strategy for Moses was threefold.

1. Moses was to have authority over his chosen helpers in that he was to be the people's representative before God (Ex. 18:19-20).
2. He was to teach the people the law of God.
3. He was to recruit capable men to aid in the ministry of caring for others.

Jethro instructed Moses that his duty was to stay out of the mundane affairs of his people and focus on being the spiritual leader. He was to devote himself to the promotion of God's glory among the people and leave the day-to-day matters to others. As a spiritual leader, he would not be overtaxed with the burden of the mundane, which would rob him of the time he needed to give to things of eternal significance.

The account of Jethro and his advice to Moses points out four basic lessons in avoiding an attempt to do God's work alone: (1) there are great dangers in the acts of one person trying to do too much; (2) the minister must know that the Lord's work is not just the work of one person, but of many; (3) a person can attempt to do so much that he does not do anything well, and (4) organized activity within the church is not necessarily unspiritual. (Jeanne Guyon, *The Way Out Paperback*, Seedsowers, 1993, pages 77-78) This last point is one that is often ignored by many church leaders who have a tendency to interpret a strong organization as being unspiritual. In fact, it can be one of the great signs that church leaders are in touch with who they are. They are humans in need of assistance. They are not God.

A PATH TO TEAM DEVELOPMENT: 7 BASIC PRINCIPLES

7 Basic Principles of The Jethro Ministry

■ ■ ■

The First Step: Defining the Roles of Church Leaders

The Jethro Ministry is designed to bring the pastoral ministry, deacon ministry and lay ministry of the congregation together. The goal is that the pastor and deacons view themselves as a cooperative group. Without this step, *The Jethro Ministry* will never take place. The pastoral staff and deacons of the fellowship must be the first to unite in an effort to shepherd the fellowship.

What Can Happen When The Jethro Ministry Is Done Correctly?

The development of a team ministry is an attempt to become more biblical in doing

> Moses' father-in-law replied, "What you are doing is not good. You and these people who come to you will only wear yourselves out. The work is too heavy for you; you cannot handle it alone.
>
> Exodus 18:17-18

ministry. The goal is to define the work of the church with words and terminologies that offer the best scriptural representation of what ministry is about.

The goal of healthy congregations should be to become a *fellowship* of Christians that practice healthy teamwork. So, how is healthy teamwork created? How can *The Jethro Ministry* become a productive and spiritually led ministry?

7 Steps for The Jethro Ministry Team Development

In creating a strategy for *The Jethro Ministry,* there are three major goals: 1) What role will the pastor and church leaders play in *The Jethro Ministry*? 2) What is the scriptural foundation for team development within *The Jethro Ministry*? and 3) How will the participation of team members within the church be encouraged by The Jethro Ministry? Under these three goals, there are seven steps to develop and deploy a productive ministry. The seven steps for any church that desires to create *The Jethro Ministry* team are:

1. Define a God-given vision
2. Demands of the vision versus the desires of others
3. Discern the urgent
4. Design a strategy that will transfer vision into team development
5. Develop the team of apprentices
6. Depend upon teammates
7. Deploy the team.

These seven steps were created to enable the congregation to have a way to evaluate and implement team development. This guideline is a strategy that connects the visionary leader with those he leads. The structure of *The Jethro Ministry* strategy has the solid support of scripture: Exodus 18. It is one thing to say to the congregation, "I have a vision!" and yet another to say, "I have a vision that is given by God and guided by scripture!"

The first objective of these seven principles is defining the vision of the leader. What is the objective of this ministry? Without the vision of the leader clarified, it is impossible to design a strategy for team development. The leader must have a clear and defined understanding as to what his objectives are. Step one is a personal phase.

Step 1: Defining a God-Given Vision for The Jethro Ministry: The Personal Phase

The creation of a healthy ministry cannot take place without clear leadership and a game plan that is understood by everyone. The direction of an organization cannot be known or understood without the direction of the leader being understood. For *The Jethro Ministry* to succeed the vision of the pastor and key leaders must be clear.

The first goal of key church leaders is to define a vision in a clear fashion and begin the process of conveying it to others. In essence, "What is the plan?" Relaying the plan can never be conveyed to the team until the one leading has a clear understanding of the plan. This will call on the pastor to lead the way. George Barna says:

> "While it is the task of the pastor to discern and articulate the vision for the church's ministry, it is imperative that the people comprehend and implement the vision in tangible ways. When the pastor alone champions the vision, the church suffers; when the people own the vision, the church thrives. The pastor is the initial disseminator of the vision. When the church is truly healthy, the pastor becomes the protector of the integrity of the vision while the people become champions of the vision."

> When the church is truly healthy, the pastor becomes the protector of the integrity of the vision while the people become champions of the vision.
>
> ***George Barna***

(George Barna, *Turn Around Churches*, Ventura, CA: Regal, 1993, page 63)

Is the vision of the church clear to the people you are leading? Do you know what God has asked you to do? Before a ministry strategy is designed, the congregation and pastor must be able to answer these two questions. In answering these two questions, the vision of the pastor and congregation must have six clear, key components.

1. First, the vision must be clear and understandable to anyone introduced to it.
2. The vision must call for action. Does it challenge those who hear it?
3. The vision should create a mental picture in the minds of those who hear it.
4. The vision is a prophetic image of what the future holds for the church.

> For God is not a God of confusion.....
> 1 Corinthians 14:33

5. A true, clear vision is built upon reality. It has a firmness to it. It does not waffle.
6. A clear vision is compelling. It possesses an energy that drives the pastor and congregation to action. (Aubrey Malphurs, *Pouring New Wine Into Old Wineskins* Grand Rapids: Baker Books, 1993, page 134)

A Path to Team Development

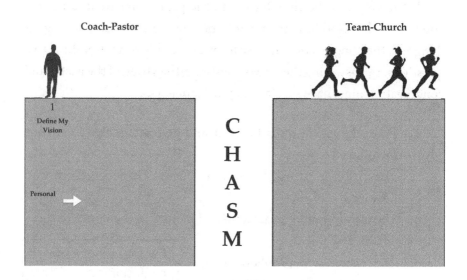

Step 2: Demands of the Vision Versus the Desires of Others for The Jethro Ministry: The Prioritizing Phase

The demands of the vision, in step one, will continually be confronted with the desires and plans of other people. The pastor and ministry team must define what is most important. What tasks and commitments take precedence over all other events? The ability to move from this step to step 3 will call upon the church leadership to ask three questions:

1. Are people asking me to work against (in a different direction) what God is asking me to do?
2. Are the demands of other people challenging my vision?
3. Are the demands of other people suppressing my vision?

If the answer is "yes" to one or all three of these questions, the pastor and church leaders will need to spend time in this step before moving on.

If the vision of the church is not clear, it will be difficult if not impossible to continue forward in the process of team development. In clarifying the demands of the vision as they confront the desires of others a simple analysis could be beneficial:

List the tasks that you do most often. These are the tasks that consume your time and energy.

> Where there is no vision, the people perish: but he that keeps the law, happy is he.
>
> Proverbs 29:18

1. Do these tasks support and agree with your God given vision?
2. If not, some time will be needed to clarify the vision before the church can proceed to the next step.
3. A helpful question at this point would be, "Why do I invest my life, energy, and resources into tasks that do not support the vision God has given me?" At this point issues that deal with the expectations of others must be addressed.

A Path to Team Development

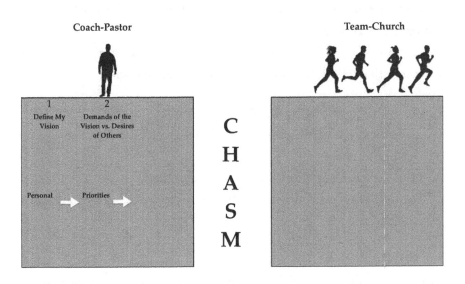

125

Step 3: Discerning the Urgent of The Jethro Ministry: The Planning Phase

> Trust in the LORD with all your heart and lean not on your own understanding; in all your ways submit to him, and he will make your paths straight. Proverbs 3:5-6

Discerning what is urgent is a cyclical step for the congregation. This step will repeat itself often during the ministry of any church. Deciding what is important will be a process that must be defined every day for church leaders. This is a point where the church must decide what will take up their time. The time and energy consumed by events and busy schedules can cripple the creation of healthy teamwork. A vision cannot grow into team development if it is jammed into an overloaded schedule of events. This means that the church will have to decide to start doing some ministries and stop doing other things that consume time and energy.

Discerning the urgent will call upon the church family to embrace that which supports the God-given vision for the fellowship and to release some responsibilities. This "releasing" does not appear to be easy for many congregations and pastors. To define what is of the utmost importance and giving it priority is the only way a team leader will be able to engage a progressive strategy.

To move forward in healthy ministry a congregation, along with the leaders in that fellowship, must ask a few simple questions:

1. What are we being asked to do?
2. Does this agree with what God has given us as a vision to accomplish?
3. Are we attempting to do this task together?
4. Are we certain that this is being driven by the design and plan of God?

When church leaders come to a clear understanding of the vision of the team, the demands of vision over the desires of other people, and is clear to what is urgent, he is ready to move into the area of the development of a strategy. Trying to develop a team ministry before the leaders of the congregation are ready will cripple the next process.

A Path to Team Development

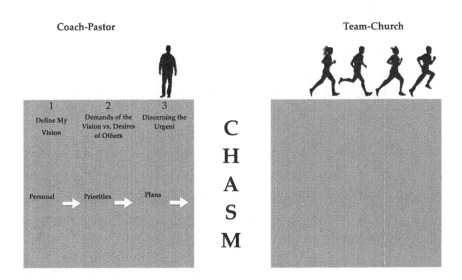

Step 4: The S.T.R.A.T.E.G.Y. of The Jethro Ministry: The Play Book Phase

When the leaders of the church understand their vision and what is urgent is to take place, the next step is to design a strategy. This strategic plan will be able to overpower the chasm that most leaders experience in team development. This step builds a bridge over the chasm between the leaders and team members. The design of a strategy is to develop teams that will enable the vision to become a reality. Developing teams without a strategic visionary plan is futile. Aubrey Malphurs puts it this way:

> "An organizational ministry vision is a must. No church
> will survive…without a single, focused vision. To attempt

ministry without a significant, well-articulated vision is to invite ministry disaster. The primary reason is that a vision provides a ministry with direction. It answers the questions - Where is this church going? What will it look like two, five, or ten years from now? The church without a clear vision is going nowhere. Few would climb on board a cruise ship if the captain had no idea where he was going. How is the church any different? A vision is also critical to other factors such as the church's unity, motivation, finances, and evaluation." (Aubrey Malphurs, *Pouring New Wine Into Old Wineskins*, pages 133-134)

Scripture is the building material to connect the team. A scriptural foundation does not only support a vision, it is the fuel that ignites the fire in the first place. It connects the visionary with the implementation of his vision. To convey a vision the pastor and team must create a strategy that is built upon the revelation of God's Word.

Without a scriptural foundation as the starting point, a congregation would find itself attempting to develop a strategy based upon personal opinion, ideology, and beliefs. A fellowship that desires to do well can begin with the advice of Jethro to Moses in Exodus and create a S.T.R.A.T.E.G.Y. built upon God's Word.

> For the word of God is living and active, sharper than any two-edged sword, piercing to the division of soul and of spirit, of joints and of marrow, and discerning the thoughts and intentions of the heart.
> Hebrews 4:12

S.T.R.A.T.E.G.Y.

1. *S-criptural foundation* for team development: No plan or strategy, regardless of its creative nature, will be stronger than the Word of God.

2. ***T-arget strengths*** to grow the team: The task of any congregation calls for an analysis of those given by God to lead. "Does someone have the gifts and talents needed to help fulfill the vision? Can this person become a team player and help accomplish the call that God has placed upon the church?"

3. ***R-ecognize obvious weaknesses***: No congregation is perfect. There are some weaknesses that cannot be escaped. What is obviously lacking? What are the strengths? Placing the right people in the right places is necessary for strong team development. This recognition does not necessarily mean that the person has mastered all the skills needed, but it does require someone who will work in the team process.

4. ***A-rrange talents***: Put the right people in the right spots. Do not allow the desire to accomplish a task in a hurry lead to misplacing someone in the wrong spot.

> Do not allow the desire to accomplish a task in a hurry lead to misplacing someone in the wrong spot.

5. ***T-each, Train, Tutor***: The congregation with a vision must take time to coach the people. The ministry development of the church must be a priority along with the preaching of God's Word.

6. ***E-nlist potential and future players***: Never stop recruiting future team members.

7. ***G-row personal relationships with team members***. The selection of a few followers and their development follows the example of Jesus. Following the example of Jesus is foundational for teamwork success.

8. ***Y-earn for success***. Wanting the church to do well and praying for its success should be the practice of every church team member. Faithful team members yearn for success.

A Path to Team Development

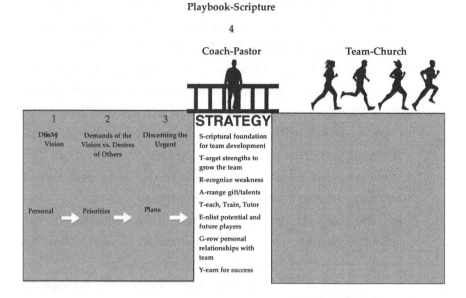

Playbook-Scripture

4

Coach-Pastor   Team-Church

1	2	3	STRATEGY
Define My Vision	Demands of the Vision vs. Desires of Others	Discerning the Urgent	S-criptural foundation for team development
			T-arget strengths to grow the team
			R-ecognize weakness
			A-rrange gift/talents
Personal →	Priorities →	Plans →	T-each, Train, Tutor
			E-nlist potential and future players
			G-row personal relationships with team
			Y-earn for success

Step 5: Development of the Team for The Jethro Ministry: The Positioning Phase

The next step for the pastor and congregation who have a vision and a clear strategy for *The Jethro Ministry* is to grow and develop this ministry. The goal is to create a team that will take the vision and fulfill the task. This positioning phase of *The Jethro Ministry* sets goals to:

Follow the example of Jesus by recruiting the Simon Peter, Andrew, James, and John of the team

- Develop a prayer support team that will help pray for the development of this ministry

> After this the Lord appointed seventy-two others and sent them two by two ahead of him to every town and place where he was about to go.
> Luke 10:1

- Select team participation as Moses was encouraged by Jethro. (Exodus 18). The overall goal here is to find those who are willing to be trained.

- Spend time in the training of those willing to be part of *The Jethro Ministry*.
- This step aims to create team dependency.

These facts should be shared with the church leaders in the early stages of *The Jethro Ministry* development:

- The Bible endorses team development.
- No more "superheroes" will be needed if we work together.
- True community will develop through the strategies of Jethro.
- The staff and church members will experience less stress if we work as a team.
- Greater synergy (the use of all gifts) evolves when we have a unified plan.
- More innovation will take place in the church when we work in harmony.
- Greater joy will be experienced by more people when we work as a team.
- The priesthood of believers becomes stronger when creating teamwork.
- Team development will facilitate healthy numerical growth for the church.
- Teams relieve the senior pastor of many responsibilities and allow him to prepare himself for the spiritual leadership of the church. (George Barna, *Building Effective Lay Leadership Team*, pages 60-67).

For *The Jethro Ministry* to be successful, creating and maintaining a team mentality is necessary. The pastor must lead the way to accept and adapt to a team approach before the congregation can respond in a productive fashion. Every pastor must realize that no team will be successful upon his guidance alone. Here are 7 C's that can help find good team members to help in the development of this ministry:

- Find someone who is willing to work as a team member. The development of *The Jethro Ministry* will require that the pastor and church leaders set the example of **cooperation.**
- The pastor must be clear with his first team member(s) what the goal of *The Jethro Ministry* will be. **Clarity** is essential.
- In the development of *The Jethro Ministry* change must be discussed early on in the process. **Change** will be inevitable for a successful ministry. The church must find those who are willing to change.
- In the development of *The Jethro Ministry* commitment must be discussed from the beginning. Without a **commitment**, it will be virtually impossible to accomplish the goals of this ministry.
- *The Jethro Ministry* team leaders must learn to **coordinate** the present situation and the desired goals. The present situation of a church cannot be ignored. It must be dealt with, but it cannot overshadow the vision and goals of this ministry.
- *The Jethro Ministry* team leaders will also need to verbally and publicly **communicate** about the task at hand. Positive and scripture based conversations must take place. Negative comments will tear down this ministry effort.
- *The Jethro Ministry* team leaders need to establish a sense of **control** within the ministry. This control is not meant to be bossy or overbearing but rather to give a sense of stability to the entire congregation. Chaos in a team will lead to its destruction.

In its purest and simplest definition, *The Jethro Ministry* is about bringing out the best in team members and stepping aside and letting the team become a unified organization. This type of process will help team members understand their positions. This type of behavior brings the church leaders and the church team to step six.

A Path to Team Development

Playbook-Scripture

4

Coach-Pastor

Coach-Pastor

Team-Church

1	2	3	STRATEGY	5
Define My Vision	Demands of the Vision vs. Desires of Others	Discerning the Urgent	S-criptural foundation for team development	Development of the Team
			T-arget strengths to grow the team	
			R-ecognize weakness	
			A-rrange gift/talents	
Personal →	Priorities →	Plans →	T-each, Train, Tutor	Positions →
			E-nlist potential and future players	
			G-row personal relationships with team	
			Y-earn for success	

Step 6: Dependency on Teammates in The Jethro Ministry: The Purpose Phase

After recruiting team players and conveying the strategy for the team, the church leaders will then be called to take another major step. The church leaders at this point need to transfer responsibility to the team to fulfill the task. This transference of authority will call upon the pastor to stand on the sideline and coach from a distance. Micromanaging simply will not work in *The Jethro Ministry*. The team members must become dependent upon one another. This step is an attempt to begin the process that will develop a clear understanding as to the team purpose. This process can be understood when the purpose of counting on one another is made clear. *The Jethro Ministry* is not a solo act.

The pastor-coach can do only so much. Every team member must be willing and wanting to grow in the task at hand. Until all the team members care about the mission, there is little hope that it will become a strong and productive effort.

The Jethro Ministry strategy must be written down, drawn out, and repeated. Organizing communication skills is a process that *The Jethro Ministry* must possess. The pastor and leaders cannot articulate what the strategy is all about and move toward surrendering that strategy to the others if communication is unclear. Having a "vision" and a "team purpose" and implementing both are essential at this point. A successful leader will focus on making the vision clear. The church leader's major goal is to increase competence in ministry. Competency cannot be accomplished without a clear understanding of the mission and strategy. Jethro had both a "vision" and a "team purpose" that he shared with Moses. He made it clear to Moses that he would have to depend on other men to help him accomplish this vision. Read again the advice that Jethro gave Moses –

"Moses' father-in-law replied, "What you are doing is not good. You and these people who come to you will only wear yourselves out. The work is too heavy for you; you cannot handle it alone. Listen now to me and I will give you some advice, and may God be with you. You must be the people's representative before God and bring their disputes to him. Teach them his decrees and instructions, and show them the way they are to live and how they are to behave. But select capable men from all the people—men who fear God, trustworthy men who hate dishonest gain—and appoint them as officials over thousands, hundreds, fifties and tens. Have them serve as judges for the people at all times, but have them bring every difficult case to you; the simple cases they can decide themselves. That will make your load lighter, because they will share it with you. If you do this and God so commands, you will be able to stand the strain, and all these people will go home satisfied." (Exodus 18:17-23, NIV)

> If you do this and God so commands, you will be able to stand the strain, and all these people will go home satisfied.

Along with defining a team purpose and being dependent upon teammates there are some attitude adjustments that must take place for *The Jethro Ministry* to be successful.

1. ***Acquiring new knowledge.*** The team members of *The Jethro Ministry* will never come to a point of possessing all knowledge. Teams are necessary because they bring a wealth of human experiences into the group. The accumulation of ministry knowledge must be an effort that is practiced by both the pastor and those leading and all team members.

2. ***Adding skills.*** You never learn to ride a bike completely until the training wheels are removed. Training wheels are necessary for a while but they must be taken off at some time. Adding new skills will be awkward and painful at times but it will be necessary if *The Jethro Ministry* team is to grow and develop. Experience, success, mistakes and failure will continue to develop this ministry.

3. ***Attitude adjustment.*** Attitude is probably the greatest adjustment in team dependency. The history of the church has made it very difficult for pastors to back off and let go. There is also the attitude in many churches that "ministry and taking care of the church is what we pay the pastor to do." The history of some churches and the expectations placed upon the pastor by some congregations and the pastors themselves have stifled team development. For *The Jethro Ministry* to work the advice of Jethro to Moses can never be forgotten, "You cannot do it alone." (Exodus 18:18, NASB)

4. ***Accountability to the team.*** The team itself will become the entity of accountability. The support given by *The Jethro Ministry* team members will determine if the team will be successful or not.

The overall goal of step six is to help every person on the team to understand their individual purpose without destroying their dependency on their teammates.

A Path to Team Development

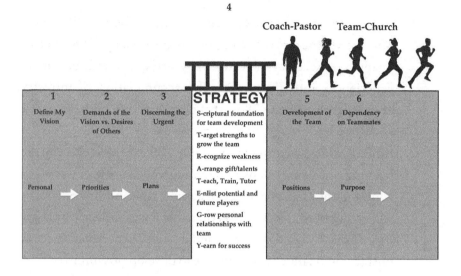

Playbook-Scripture

4

Coach-Pastor   Team-Church

1	2	3	STRATEGY	5	6
Define My Vision	Demands of the Vision vs. Desires of Others	Discerning the Urgent	S-criptural foundation for team development	Development of the Team	Dependency on Teammates
			T-arget strengths to grow the team		
			R-ecognize weakness		
			A-rrange gift/talents		
			T-each, Train, Tutor		
Personal →	Priorities →	Plans →	E-nlist potential and future players	Positions →	Purpose →
			G-row personal relationships with team		
			Y-earn for success		

Step 7: Deployment of The Jethro Ministry: The Performing Phase

In this last step, the goal is to *deploy* a ministry team (This will be discussed in the next chapter). When *The Jethro Ministry Team* is ready for deployment there are certain characteristics that will show. The following takes place when this team is ready to go to work:

1. The team members can clearly define the purpose of *The Jethro Ministry* to anyone.
2. They should be able to tell why the team exists.
3. They should be able to define the mission of the team.
4. Team members should know the priorities of the team.
5. Team members should know their "roles" on the team.
6. Each member should recognize when someone else can preform a task better. This realization will be a time to give tasks away to those who can accomplish the task.

7. At this level members regard team meetings as necessary. A good team will not have to beg its members to attend.

8. At this level team members are respective to feedback and opportunities to update, grow, change, and increase their skills.

9. At this level team members understand that conflicts will arise. In fact, conflicts are to be expected. Dealing with conflict is a spiritual matter. Calling on the power of the Holy Spirit and depending on the Bible for guidance will help deal with conflict.

A Path to Team Development

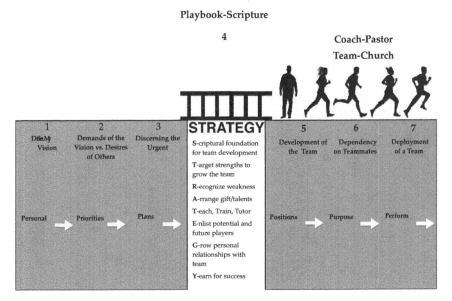

Playbook-Scripture

4

Coach-Pastor
Team-Church

1	2	3	STRATEGY	5	6	7
Define My Vision	Demands of the Vision vs. Desires of Others	Discerning the Urgent	S-criptural foundation for team development	Development of the Team	Dependency on Teammates	Deployment of a Team
			T-arget strengths to grow the team			
			R-ecognize weakness			
			A-rrange gift/talents			
Personal →	Priorities →	Plans →	T-each, Train, Tutor	Positions →	Purpose →	Perform →
			E-nlist potential and future players			
			G-row personal relationships with team			
			Y-earn for success			

The Jethro Ministry is all about healthy teamwork but this ministry cannot take place without a clear understanding of what a good team looks like. When a church group is ready to grow as a team, they are ready to embrace the ministry strategy that Jethro gave to Moses.

The next chapter is a basic guideline on how to build and activate *The Jethro Ministry*.

HOW TO BUILD THE JETHRO MINISTRY

How to Build the Jethro Ministry

■ ■ ■

So often the needs of the local church lead the congregation to enlist more deacons to handle the demands of ministry. For many fellowships, this has proven to be a problem. Issues of deacon qualifications or the lack of those willing to serve can prove to be difficult issues for many fellowships. The number of deacons to care for a fellowship is not the answer. The quality of leadership is the key. In other words, *The Jethro Ministry* can lead a congregation, with a few gifted leaders to be able to minister to many people.

Leaders of Ten

When Jethro gave Moses advice on how to care for God's people, he suggested that Moses break down the responsibility of taking care of the people. He told Moses,

> "You be the people's representative before God, and you bring the disputes to God, then teach them the statutes and the laws, and make known to them the way in which they are to walk and the work they are to do. Furthermore,

you shall select out of all the people able men who fear God, men of truth, those who hate dishonest gain; and you shall place *these* over them *as* leaders of thousands, of hundreds, of fifties and of tens." (Exodus 18:19-21, NASB)

The first rule for deacons in *The Jethro Ministry* is that they are directly responsible for *a maximum of ten people*. Upon this statement is where many churches will lay this book down and say that this is an unrealistic plan. However, what is unrealistic is to believe that any one man, with a family, a job, and any amount of time to himself can minister to more people than the Lord Jesus chose as His disciples. Jesus taught as much by example as He did by His words. There was a reason that Jesus recruited twelve men to follow him. The dynamics of human communication and the skills to build personal relationships decreases when more people are added to the group. Even though Jesus was the Son of God and had the ability to heal, turn water into wine, and raise a man from the dead, he showed by his example how important it is to train, encourage and empower people on a small scale.

There is something significant in the manner in which Jesus taught. Many pastors, theologians, and church leaders have separated ministry and disciple making. The two cannot be separated. Therefore, if a congregation wishes to minister well, following the example of how Jesus dealt with His disciples is essential.

The following diagram gives an idea of how effective a deacon's ministry can be if the church follows the example set up for Moses by Jethro. If one deacon was responsible for only ten people and those ten people were willing to minister to five people, the results would look something like this:

The Jethro Ministry

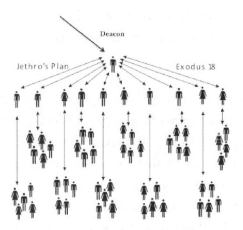

As shown above, the deacon is the one person at the top of the graph. The ten people below the one deacon are **10 Caregivers of The Jethro Ministry**. This strategy calls for each deacon never to have more than 10 Caregivers. The goal of The Jethro Ministry is to create a healthy and productive team of caregivers within the fellowship.

The Caregivers who work under the leadership of the deacon will be asked to find and recruit 5 Prayer Partners through their network of people within the congregation.

When a Deacon has 10 Caregivers and each Caregiver has 5 Prayer Partners this will mean that 1 Deacon will be connecting to 60 people. This set-up will complete that deacon's network of responsibility.

When this set-up takes place, the church can effectively minister with as few as 5 deacons when attendance/membership is less than 305 people (see pages 144-145). The number of deacons needed to make *The Jethro Ministry* effective will depend upon the size of the congregation.

How can The Jethro Ministry work in your church?

As already established in this book, teamwork is essential in developing a healthy ministry. Teamwork can become a powerful tool for the success and growth of any Christian fellowship. To make *The Jethro Ministry* work it must be built upon three basic ministry teams:

1. The Deacon Team
2. The Caregiver Team
3. The Prayer Partner Team

The Deacon Team:

For The Jethro Ministry to be successful, the deacons must be seen as a ministry team, not a "board of directors." (Acts 6:1-7) The first and greatest responsibility of the deacons is to be sure that The Jethro Ministry (Exodus 18) is understood as caring for the fellowship. All other responsibilities of deacons take second place to caring for the church family. This ministry strategy will call a congregations to reorganize the structure of ministry that Jethro led Moses to develop.

It starts with the deacons.

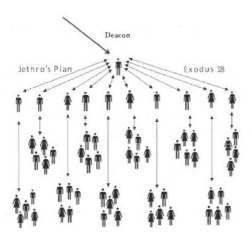

The Jethro Ministry is a ministry strategy that understands that people have limitations, just like Moses had limitations. (Exodus 18:17-18) *No deacon will ever have more than 10 individual Caregivers* for which they are <u>directly responsible.</u> When all the deacons have 10 Caregivers the church will seek another deacon to be added to the list of active deacons. The main responsibility of the deacons is to develop a relationship with the Caregivers under their leadership and stay in contact with them.

The first goal that the deacons encourage their Caregivers to accomplish is that of finding 5 Prayer Partners to join them in *The Jethro Ministry*. This effort looks like this:

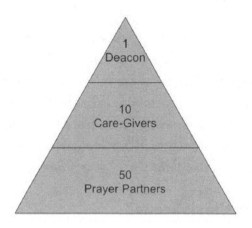

When One Deacon Ministers to Ten Caregivers

Key: The maximum number of Caregivers for any deacon is 10 people. The maximum Prayer Partners for each Caregiver is 5. If this strategy is followed carefully the results will create an environment of healthy teamwork development within the congregation.

1 Deacons + 10 Caregivers + 50 Prayer Partners = 61 People

5 Deacons + 50 Caregivers + 250 Prayer Partners = 305 People

10 Deacons + 100 Caregivers + 500 Prayer Partners = 610 People

15 Deacons + 150 Caregivers + 750 Prayer Partners = 915 People

20 Deacons + 200 Caregivers + 1000 Prayer Partners = 1220 People

25 Deacons + 250 Caregivers + 1250 Prayers Partners = 1525 People

30 Deacons + 300 Caregivers + 1500 Prayer Partners = 1830 People

50 Deacons + 500 Caregivers + 2500 Prayer Partners = 3050 People

The Caregivers

The Caregivers are connected to the Deacons of the church. Each Caregiver will be connected to one active deacon. The Caregivers are the laity of the congregation who answered the call of God to help "care" for the church family.

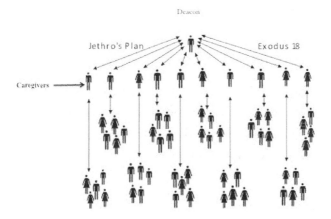

The overall goal of Caregivers is to stay in contact with their deacon and to recruit five Prayer Partners to pray for the ministry and mission of the fellowship. No Caregiver of *The Jethro Ministry* has more than 5 people for which they are to partner with as "Prayer Partners."

Each Caregiver will contact those under their care on a regular basis. Some Caregivers will find telephone calls to be the best form of contact while others may use text messaging or emails. The way contacts are made between Caregivers and Prayer Partners will depend upon the personalities in each group.

Here are some Bible verses to support those who have agreed to be *Caregivers* in *The Jethro Ministry*:

> **Philippians 2:1-4, NIV** - Therefore if you have any encouragement from being united with Christ, if any comfort from his love, if any common sharing in the Spirit, if any tenderness and compassion, then make my joy complete by being like-minded, having the same love, being one in spirit and of one mind. Do nothing out of selfish ambition or vain conceit. Rather, in humility value others above yourselves, not looking to your own interests but each of you to the interests of the others.

■ ■ ■

> **John 13:34-35, NIV** - A new command I give you: Love one another. As I have loved you, so you must love one another. By this everyone will know that you are my disciples, if you love one another.

■ ■ ■

> **1 John 3:18, NIV** - Dear children, let us not love with words or speech but with actions and in truth.

■ ■ ■

> **Ephesian 4:32, NIV** - Be kind and compassionate to one another, forgiving each other, just as in Christ God forgave you.

The Prayer Partner

Prayer Partners of *The Jethro Ministry* are those individuals who have answered God's call to pray for the ministry and fellowship of their church.

Prayer Partners are those who take a conversational prayer life with the Lord very seriously. The task of the Prayer Partners is to approach the Throne of God on behalf of the church and the congregation. For *The Jethro Ministry* to be successful, prayer must be foundational to every aspect of this ministry. Real success will only take place when the team prays faithfully.

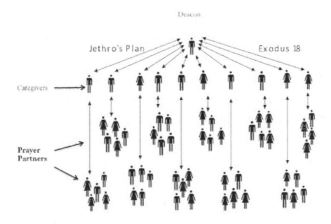

Bible Verses to Support The Jethro Ministry Prayer Partners

"About eight days after Jesus said this, he took Peter, John and James with him and went up onto a mountain to pray." - Luke 9:28, NIV

"Watch and pray so that you will not fall into temptation. The spirit is willing, but the body is weak." - Mark 14:32, NIV

"And I will do whatever you ask in my name, so that the Father may be glorified in the Son." – John 14:13, NIV

"Do not be anxious about anything, but in every situation, by prayer and petition, with thanksgiving, present your requests to God. And the peace of God, which transcends all understanding, will guard your hearts and your minds in Christ Jesus.- Philippians 4:6-7, NIV

"Rejoice always, pray continually, give thanks in all circumstances; for this is God's will for you in Christ Jesus.- 1 Thessalonians 5:16-18, NIV

Is anyone among you in trouble? Let them pray. Is anyone happy? Let them sing songs of praise. Is anyone among you sick? Let them call the elders of the church to pray over them and anoint them with oil in the name of the Lord. And the prayer offered in faith will make the sick person well; the Lord will raise them up. If they have sinned, they will be forgiven." - James 5:13-15, NIV

This is the confidence we have in approaching God: that if we ask anything according to his will, he hears us. ¹⁵ And if we know that he hears us—whatever we ask—we know that we have what we asked of him.- 1 John 5:14-15, NIV

How to Keep the Jethro Ministry Effective

- The deacons will meet monthly
- Training will be provided each year for all "Caregivers" involved in *The Jethro Ministry*
- PRAYER is the essential foundation for *The Jethro Ministry* to succeed.

- The overall goal for the church is to pray with and for those under their care, and the Caregivers to pray with and for those under their care.

- Each member of *The Jethro Ministry* will make a "Covenant" at the beginning of each ministry year.

Covenant for The Jethro Ministry

The Jethro Ministry is a unified ministry effort between the pastoral staff, deacons, and laity to be sure that every person that makes up the fellowship is personally contacted and prayed for. The ministry covenant can be accomplished with 7 basic steps.

1. Make contact with those in your care group.

The overriding goal of *The Jethro Ministry* is to create a fluid contact ministry between the Deacons, Caregivers, Prayer Partners and the Ministry Team of the church. These contacts are made between the Deacons and Caregivers and from the Caregivers to those in their Prayer Group. Contacts can be done in person or by phone, text messaging, or email.

2. Become an important PIECE of the puzzle that helps create the ministry structure.

Without every Deacon and Caregiver and Prayer Partner involved in *The Jethro Ministry*, the team structure will not be complete. Everyone is a significant piece to the puzzle. As a **"PIECE"** of *The Jethro Ministry* every member of the team plays an important role in the overall ministry of the church by:

> Praying with those you care for.
> Identify with those you care for.
> Encourage those you care for.
> Cultivate friendships with those you care for.
> Edify (spiritually instructing) those you care for.

3. Help grow and nurture friendships in your Care Group.

The goal of The Jethro Ministry is to follow the example of Jesus in ministry. Jesus told his disciples,

> "I no longer call you servants, because a servant does not know his master's business. Instead, I have called you friends, for everything that I learned from my Father I have made known to you. You did not choose me, but I chose you and appointed you so that you might go and bear fruit—fruit that will last—and so that whatever you ask in my name the Father will give you. This is my command: Love each other." (John 15:15-17, NIV)

4. Support Bible Study and Small Groups

> "And let us consider how we may spur one another on toward love and good deeds, not giving up meeting together, as some are in the habit of doing, but encouraging one another—and all the more as you see the Day approaching." (Hebrews 10:24-25, NIV)

> "Therefore encourage one another and build each other up, just as in fact you are doing." (1 Thessalonians 5:11, NIV)

> "For where two or three gather in my name, there am I with them." (Matthew 18:20, NIV)

5. Pray for the Church Leaders

Paul gives some advice on how to pray for church leaders.

> "For this reason, since the day we heard about you, we have not stopped praying for you. We continually ask God to fill you with the knowledge of his will through all

the wisdom and understanding that the Spirit gives, ..."
(Colossians 1:9, NIV)

"Now we ask you, brothers and sisters, to acknowledge those who work hard among you, who care for you in the Lord and who admonish you. Hold them in the highest regard in love because of their work. Live in peace with each other. (1 Thessalonians 5:12-13, NIV)

"For this reason, ever since I heard about your faith in the Lord Jesus and your love for all God's people, I have not stopped giving thanks for you, remembering you in my prayers. [17] I keep asking that the God of our Lord Jesus Christ, the glorious Father, may give you the Spirit of wisdom and revelation, so that you may know him better." (Ephesians 1:15-17, NIV)

6. Attend The Jethro Ministry training courses when offered.

7. Pray for the Jethro Ministry.

My Covenant Agreement to The Jethro Ministry:

I understand and support **The Jethro Ministry**.

I will do my best, with the Lord's help, to be a faithful Deacon/Caregiver of **The Jethro Ministry**.

I also agree to be an encourager and prayer partner with all who have agreed to this covenant.

(your name)   (date)

Some Helpful Suggestions and Tools to Assist in The Jethro Ministry

What are the characteristics of a healthy Deacon, Caregiver and Prayer Partner who are involved in the Jethro Ministry?

Healthy Deacons, Caregivers and Prayer Partners:

- Are faithful in their spiritual growth.
- Are those that study the Bible on a regular basis.
- Are encouragers of those under their care.
- Contact those under their care on a regular basis.
- Become friends of those whom they care about.
- Grow in ministry, in all seasons, from joy to sorrow.
- Grow as praying people.
- Grow as communicators of the ministries of the church.

This last statement brings us to three basic tools of communication for *The Jethro Ministry* to be successful. The three basic tools of communication can help empower *The Jethro Ministry*:

1. Telephone Contacts
2. Text or Email Contacts
3. Personal Contacts

Telephone/Cell Phone Contacts

Be sure your call is built around more than an invitation to Bible Study or Worship. Here are helpful ideas for phone contacts:

- A get acquainted call.
- An invitation to become "prayer partners".
- Follow up on prayer concerns.
- Share upcoming church events.

- Wish a happy birthday, anniversary, etc...
- Share a holiday wish or greeting.
- "How are you doing?" call.

Never give the impression that you are after something from the person you are calling. Remember, there is a big difference between a "Caregiver" and a "Caretaker".

Reasons to email or text:

- Remember special occasions.
- Send an invitation to events and church-wide functions
- Let the person know that you are praying for them.
- Send a Bible verse that has spoken to you.
- Send a website link that you have found helpful.
- Birthday
- Anniversary
- Get Well

Personal Contacts (Visit)

A personal contact or visit would be a time to nurture a growing friendship. It is not necessary to "talk church" during your visit. If the opportunity arises to talk about the Lord and the church take this time as one sent from the Lord. Let the Spirit lead.

Personal contacts can happen:
- On the golf course
- In an exercise class
- During a ball game
- Over lunch
- At a community gathering
- In the grocery store

- At the post office
- Anywhere outside of a church event or off church property.

Take advantage of every opportunity you may have to nurture a caring relationship. Taking the time is the key to being successful in the area of personal contacts.

Can The Jethro Ministry Work in Your Fellowship?

Not too many years ago I witnessed a congregation drop in attendance to less than 5 members. Several pastors were willing to work with the fellowship only to discover that the few members left did not want to follow their guidance. After several years of trying to decide what to do, the few members who were left decided to sell their property to the local university. The university bought the property for one dollar; that's right, *one dollar*! How can a church get in that kind of shape? Why does a church decline and become such a lifeless organization? Can a congregation like this ever hope for a healthy future?

I have come to believe that any congregation can experience a resurgence of new life if they are willing to work together as a team. Teamwork, led by the Lord, is the key! Church members along with the pastor must have an overpowering desire to see their church become an organization empowered by God. This type of desire is what Jethro led Moses to embrace.

For *The Jethro Ministry* to work, churches must start with a group of people willing to pray for the power of the Holy Spirit to take control. The pastor must be willing to become a leader. The congregation must be willing to care for the people who make up the fellowship.

> "If you follow this advice, and if the Lord agrees,
> you will be able to endure the pressures, and there
> will be peace and harmony in the camp."
> (Exodus 18:23)